Redefining

Success

Real Women, Real Stories,

Real Inspiration.

EDITED BY SARAH WALTON

AND ALLY NATHANIEL

ISBN: 0996287051

ISBN-13 978-0996287050

TABLE OF CONTENTS:

FORWARD

We're so glad that you've picked up this book! We hope you find the stories we've put together useful and inspiring as you venture out in the world to share the best of yourself and everything you have to offer.

We've chosen wonderful women to participate in this book and we think you'll agree with us when you've finished reading. But before you go further, let us introduce ourselves, we're Ally and Sarah and we've come together to create this collection of stories, just for you.

Ally:

A few years ago I created a new folder under the "publishing" file on my computer and named it "Women's Inspiration." I knew it was the beginning of something new, but I didn't know what that "something" was.

Less than two years after my daughter was born, I was new to the U.S. and was 100% financially dependent on my husband. I didn't have a work visa and I had three kids under the age of five. I felt lost and empty. As a forum manager and online magazine editor back in Israel, I had supported pregnant women and new moms on the biggest online communities in my home country. I invested countless hours without getting paid, and I loved it. I found my

1

modest contribution to the women's community to be very fulfilling.

But fast-forward a few years, and three kids, later, I'd spent countless hours asking myself questions about womanhood and why the hell it can feel so hard to navigate through life. I'd been told that women and men have the same rights and opportunities, but it certainly didn't feel that way. My needs, wishes, and thoughts were set to the side and I felt like there was something wrong with me for allowing that to happen. During a lunch conversation with a friend, I was lamenting my situation. She looked me in the eye and said, "You should trust your own thinking." In that moment I realized I'd completely given up my own thinking. I'd allowed my husband to pull the wagon and been too afraid to say anything. That one sentence changed my life.

Just two weeks later I'd found a job as a pastry chef, signed my daughter up for day care, and started a new phase in my life. I kept asking questions about women, men, and the world. I looked deeply into my fears, the messages I got from society as a woman and studied the differences between women and men and our behavioral patterns. I've learned so much and wanted to return to my old passion of supporting other women. I don't want any woman to feel the way I felt for most of my life. It doesn't have to be that way!

When I asked Sarah if she wanted to write a book with me, I had this idea of bringing women entrepreneurs together to share our stories. I didn't want it to be another "get rich fast" or "I will tell you what to do" book. I wanted it to be a book about real women, their fears, their painful pasts, their truncated moments, and their hopes. I wanted to show other women that there is no such thing as "overnight success" and that a big part of being successful is making the decision to make a difference.

When Sarah agreed to create this book with me, I couldn't believe it. It was a dream come true. I feel so blessed and grateful that this project has come to life, and that Sarah's part of my life now. I couldn't do it without her! *That* is the power of women.

Sarah:

I've often felt like the only woman in the room. As a child, I grew up in a house with five brothers, always the only girl. Then as I launched my career in technology, and started to climb the corporate ladder, there were fewer and fewer women around me. I ran into almost every scenario Sheryl Sandberg describes in her book *Lean In*, and while I appreciated that she started the discussion about the differences between men and women, I didn't hear many solutions. Instead, I felt more pressure, like I was reading an outline of everything women are doing wrong in the face of a business culture that doesn't work for us.

Since I've left corporate America, I've heard many "Follow me and you'll make a million dollars!" claims that target women who are searching for a paradigm outside of the standard business culture. I've also watched the massive hemorrhaging of talent from corporate America as women opt to leave because the schedule and rigid culture don't work for us. Women are looking for a new way to share their talents with the world, and we're losing our willingness to be told how that should be done. I believe the next few years will bring a shift in our corporate structure as more women become the breadwinners of the family, others leave to start their own businesses, and even more choose to stay in the "system" (as I lovingly call it). This shift will offer flexibility, fair compensation, and fluid hours, so companies can hang on to the talent that's been fleeing in droves.

When Ally first approached me about her idea for this book, I was thrilled. I knew it was important, and that people would want to read it. However, my first response was, "Oh I love that idea! But I have way too much going on." I completely underestimated Ally's passion for other women and her keen eye for the truth. She gently and persistently asked me again. And again. Soon I was so won over by her heart and mind, and how completely her mission aligned with my own, that I had no choice but to fall in love with this project and get started. It's become one of my proudest accomplishments to date.

I so love and respect the women in this book who've chosen to be honest, to be vulnerable, and to share the truth in the hopes of inspiring and comforting other women. And while no single woman can have all the answers for everyone, together, we can learn from each other, choose which traits we want to emulate, which we want to avoid, and garner insights into our own paths.

Success, despite what we've been told, is not achieved by outward markers. Those come and go, and their value to us is fleeting. This is true for everyone, but especially for women. We're told from a very young age how to act, how to be, what to wear, what to wish for, and how to behave. But rarely are we given permission to seek success for ourselves, on our own terms. My hope is that this book will offer that permission to every woman who picks it up. Your story is just that, *your* story. Success is yours to define, yours to grow, and yours to pursue.

THE MAVERICK

Raquel Ramirez

Paving your own way is always important. Learning how to do it the right way takes time, patience and faith.

I was standing in the middle of Nordstrom, as the loss prevention team handcuffed me for attempting to steal a pair of Nike running shorts and a sports bra. My rush of rebellion and adventure quickly melted away. My 19-year-old self didn't feel so cool and courageous anymore. Suddenly I felt like I was stuck in a bad dream. Kind of like that one where you show up to school naked. After a long drive to a women's facility center I made that dreadful "one call" to my house. My brother answered the phone. The worst moment of my eight hours there, even worse than all of the paperwork, was hearing the haunting words, "Raquel, no! Not you!" from my brother when

I notified him over the phone. He would be the one to show up to bail me out. We decided not to give mom a heart attack by revealing to her that her baby girl was about to spend the night in jail. She would learn about it the next morning.

I wish I could tell you I learned my lesson from that experience, but I didn't. Only a year later at my alma mater, San Diego State University (SDSU), I was held at citizen's arrest by the university's librarian for attempting to steal a communication scholarly journal from their Archives & Special Collections. It was a non-circulating material only available within this section of library. So naturally, the rebel in me thought, "Since I can't check it out, I'll just take it." Not my best decision. At my court hearing, I remember feeling both annoyed at having to be there, and scared. I was jolted to attention when the deputy district attorney looked at me and grimly declared, "You will never be able to work for the government. You really messed up."

Two things crossed my mind: "Who the heck wants to work for the government?" and "What did I just do?" Had I just closed a door on myself? I felt confused and dumbfounded.

Later that evening I lay crouched in my bed quietly crying so no one would hear me, blasting the Dixie Chicks' CD *Wide Open Spaces*. Ironically, my spaces didn't feel so wide and open anymore. I eventually fell asleep on my very damp pillow. A few days later, my friends Geri, Israel and Josie called and invited me to a church service. I had said no to them what felt like a million times before. But on this particular night, I was feeling like a loser. So when they called, I felt something tug at me to go. I went. I've come to believe that the service I attended that night was my divine appointment with God. It was during that service when I accepted Jesus as my Lord and Savior. I felt as though this service had been customized to deliver a message especially for me. The worship team started singing and the leader said, "You may think you're not enough. You may think you're not good enough or worthy because of life choices you've made, but you *are* enough. God loves you right there just as you are. He loves you and wanted you to hear that tonight. That's why you're here." I don't remember what was said after that because some woman was crying so loudly it felt like my head was going to burst. Then I realized that I was the woman.

After that night, my life was never the same. That doesn't mean that everything was rosy. I still faced trials, challenges, and feats, but the hope and joy of my faith sustained me. I started to discover my own purpose and understand more about how I was designed and my innate gifts. As I look back, the pieces of my life have become clearer and have started to make sense. The eras of my life are pieces of a larger jigsaw puzzle; and as the pieces fit together, more details

9

of the bigger picture are revealed: who I am and how I work.

It started in elementary school. Every teacher wrote a similar note with my grade card, which read something like this, "Raquel is a smart girl, but she talks too much in class." My first-grade teacher gave me double the workload to keep me busy (and quiet). So to make sure I had the time I wanted to talk, I learned how to complete my work faster. Then, in fifth grade, I made it my personal mission to compete with the class nerd to see who could finish our math assignments first. Winning was such a high for me. I didn't care so much that my work was done, and cared even less that it was done correctly. I just loved the rush of endorphins from winning the race.

At home, my family didn't understand why I couldn't just follow the rules and do things the way they did. As I grew older, they continued to be confused, as I was involved in many high school extracurricular activities: the school newspaper, musical theater, soccer, and student council. In my yearbook one of my classmates wrote, "How would our school run without you?" One evening, sitting in the living room as I was preparing my speech as part of the homecoming court, my sister Sonia walked in the room, studied me practicing, and asked, "Why are you like this? None of us were like this in school."

My parents couldn't understand why I was so driven and determined to pave my own way; but between you and me: It was their example I was following. Without speaking a word of English, having zero support system, and with only the money in their pockets, my parents ventured to the United States in the 1970s to pursue the American Dream. I know we hear that story often, but I can't imagine what that was like for them. I think sometimes we can be numb to the triumphs of others. But I certainly wasn't numb to the example my parents set for me.

As the sixth child of eight kids, I grew up watching my dad, Ruben, advance from field worker, to construction assistant, to owning his own construction company. He was my first example of an entrepreneurial life. At five foot ten my dad has a face that has always showcased a Magnum-style mustache and his looks resemble the Mexican Ranchero musician, Vicente Fernández, which he's always been secretly proud of. He worked hard, but he was always there for family vacations and holidays. He really enjoyed his craft; he even worked on projects around the house on his days off. My father provided for our family of ten and was still prepared for financial emergencies. I'm grateful that I was able to watch him work on his own terms. I gleaned a lot from him: his worth ethic, his fun sense of humor, and his dance moves. Dad was always the first and last on the dance floor at family parties. He knows how to have fun, but constantly reminds us of our responsibility to our family.

My mother, Rosario, was a stay-at-home mom who has a heart to help others and contribute to the family finances. She was a fierce sales lady for Stanley, Avon, Home Interior, Tupperware, and just about any other opportunity where she could work at home. At five feet tall, my mom is a plump figured woman with fair skin and forever-highlighted hair. She couldn't even drive, and she had eight children to look after, but that didn't keep her from contributing to the family finances and having fun at the same time. Mom didn't always appreciate our sense of humor, but her prudent and sensitive personality helped us refine our manners and etiquette.

Both my parents imparted gifts to me: From my father I received the spirit of entrepreneurship and from my mother I obtained the desire to become a stay-at-home mom. It's been a privilege to watch my parents rise from humble circumstances because they were determined that *their current situation was not their future.* And it's that same drive to succeed, and my craving for adventure, that drove me to pursue higher education – something that some of my siblings had attempted, but didn't complete. I was determined to go, thrive, and finish. This is not to say that my drive and desire for adventure wasn't misplaced at times. (Cough, cough, Nordstrom!) Sometimes I was misguided and careless with these seemingly good traits. My "inner rebel" had a hard time following rules, and I was driven to do dumb things for an endorphin rush.

I arrived at college both proud and scared. As I entered the halls of beautiful SDSU, I thought of my high school counselor who had said, "Raquel, not everyone needs to go to community college; some are ready to go straight to a university." Wow. Me? The child of Mexican immigrants who couldn't help me with my college admission papers because they could not speak, read, or write English? *I* was good enough?

My oldest sister, Lilia, helped me complete all the paperwork on time, attended orientation, and accompanied me on campus tours. She even walked the campus with me the week before I started classes to ensure I wouldn't get lost. She was as invested in my success as I was. And I know that my graduation day meant as much to her as it meant to me.

As my name was called to receive the diploma for my Bachelor of Arts in Communication, I turned to see a proud and very loud Mexican family cheering me on. They had even dressed in red, black, and white, the SDSU colors. I looked out at the crowd to find Lilia and I saw the tears in her eyes. She told me later, "When I saw you walk across the stage, I started crying because I thought of how hard you've worked to earn this." I know it wasn't just my own determination that got me there, but my loving family, too. That moment wasn't just for me; it was for all of us.

As great as that moment remained in my life, I always heard a small voice say to me, "If SDSU allowed *you* to enroll and graduate, it must not be that great of a school." Sometimes others recognize the greatness in us before we come to realize it in ourselves. And until I did, it was difficult for me to accept achievements and recognition. After finishing college I started my first full-time job as a bilingual telemarketing supervisor feeling so responsible and wise. That's where I met Rocky, my husband. The company rules didn't allow employees to date each other. But I was a rebel in every area of my life, and I didn't make work an exception.

Soon I became disillusioned with my nine-to-five job. I worked diligently; I gave it every juicy ounce of creativity I could. Fearlessly driven by new challenges, I went above and beyond the expectations of management. But the company vision was not *my* vision. That dream belonged to the man who had founded the company thirty years before. I felt like I was drying up inside and knew it was time to move on. The day I gave my resignation, my manager said, "You know, Raquel, the grass isn't always greener on the other side." This was his last earnest effort to keep a diligent worker bee like me. All I could think was, "Oh, but I plan to water it lavishly." I mean, if I could work that hard for someone else, imagine what I could do for myself!

I ventured into the real estate market in the booming years where hard work meant putting up a "For Sale" sign in the morning and selling the house by the end of the day. Starting as a volunteer in a local real estate office, I was soon hired on as the office assistant. I quickly learned the ins and outs of real estate. I worked attentively and I led with innovation and grit. However, the culture was not created by me nor cultivated by me. Once again, I was eager for the next adventure. When my colleague, and now business mentor, asked me to join him in opening our own real estate company, I jumped at the opportunity. At 28 years old, I had my own business. Opening a new real estate office was a lot of work and a lot of responsibility. But it was ours: We created the culture, developed the team, and cast the vision. What great moments these were!

In 2008, my life changed again. I gave birth to a trailblazer in his own right, Rockford. His birth coupled with the uncertainty of the real estate landscape made me feel like it was the perfect time to transition to stay-at-home-mom. The idea of returning to real estate evaporated the first day I was home with my son. The motherhood adventure has kept me filled to the brim with challenges, creative problem solving, and physical endurance. I know the walk of a mother and it's not for the faint of heart. It's a ministry, especially in the early years. I'm determined to be an extraordinary mother. It's amazing how we can give up sleep, eat last, wear puke on our sleeves, and somehow really believe we're still not good enough.

A few years later, Rockford had a little brother, and I was expecting our third child. This is when my husband suggested I consider studying to earn my master's degree in Business. It was perfect for me. I relished the learning and writing. With late nights, a newborn, and a wonderfully supportive husband, I eventually graduated and even made the honor society.

Shortly after earning a master's degree in Business Management, I discovered my calling and launched my social media consulting and management company, RMR Social Media. This job inspires me daily. While carrying out some market research for a client, I had another "aha moment" and birthed my next small business, Princess Revolution, a Christian T-shirt business for girls. The shirts convey faith with sassiness, strength, and style. What an adventure life is! It is filled with great triumphs, poor judgment calls, beautiful births, and constant change. We only get one life, and we should live it as the best version of ourselves.

I'd like to tell you that I've remained an upstanding citizen and that I'm not proud of talking my way out of 12 or 13 driving tickets, but I'd be lying. No, I haven't had an encounter with the law, but I've remained true to my inner rebel.

Later this year I'll be employed by a local school district to teach social media courses for continuing education students. Recalling how the deputy district attorney had told me I would never be able to work for the government, I have to giggle. Even those doors we close on ourselves can be reopened. Moments of recklessness and poor judgment do *not* have to define us; they can be steps that draw us closer to becoming who we are if we are willing to take the next steps.

There's been one more recent breakthrough I'd like to share. I mean one of those big power breakthroughs that only Oprah talks about. Here it is:

How we are designed does not change because of our circumstances or our environment. We are all uniquely designed.

The trick is, we have to discover that design. To help myself find mine, I read Sally Hogshead's book, *How the World Sees You*. The book explains how important it is to be uniquely *you*. I discovered that I'm a Maverick Leader who thrives on innovation and power. (You're shocked, I know.) When I first read that I add value, am quick to solve problems with fresh solutions, able to generate ideas that surprise with a new perspective, and have an ability to ditch tradition that keeps people engaged, I had to laugh out loud. Next I read the adjectives listed for how the world sees me: creative, irreverent, and entrepreneurial. I looked up the definitions of these words and I examined them like a child intently studying a new bug.

Then one night as I was taking a shower and feeling the warmth of the water trickling down my scalp, I saw all my life flash before my eyes. All those moments highlighting "how I was me" shouted out like an anthem. **How I was me had never changed, regardless of my circumstances.** I was always a creative maverick with a humble heart; I just didn't always practice discernment, and I didn't focus on the healthiest ways to fuel my maverick nature. We are all designed with a purpose and we can all use our design for good.

Have you ever noticed that a car is meticulously designed and equipped for its purpose? For example, I know that my minivan wasn't designed for a grand prix. Just like I know my husband's Lexus wasn't designed to go off-roading. I think we human beings are like that, too. I believe we're each designed and equipped for a purpose. For *our* purpose. Some of us were lucky enough to discover this early in life, for others it might take a lifetime. Me? I was more on the lifetime track.

I've learned to accept myself, just as I am. I am the maverick leader and proud of it. Before I understood this, I'd let my maverick nature lead me to break the law. Today I break barriers and convention. Before a "No" drove me to retaliate. Now it drives me to perform while remaining kind. Before I lacked focus and structure. Now I recognize the need for my creative spirit to soar.

Allowing God in my life helped me embrace my design. Throughout my life, people have told me how I was different, how I didn't follow the rules, how I didn't conform. They were right, and all this time, there has been nothing wrong with me. I was designed to be exactly who I am: a creative maverick with a humble heart. I finally understand the popular concept, "Be Unapologetically You."

I believe God used Sally Hogshead's book to speak to me just as he did in that special church service. This time the message was, "There's nothing wrong with you. I designed you just as you are. Embrace it, live it, and bless others with it." Maybe you already know how you were designed, or maybe you're still discovering it. Either way, once you find it, own it, and share it.

A note from Sarah and Ally: It's not always easy to accept our own uniqueness, especially in a world that wants us to conform. What we love so much about Raquel's story is how honest she is about the winding path she took to find her unique design. But the beauty of her story is that she didn't stop there. She could have simply embraced her maverick side and left it at that, but she didn't. She went beyond herself and shares her voice and perspective with others. She uses her talents and unique style to help her clients stand out on social media, and for young girls to stand out, in a positive way, not in a cleavage, belly-button exposing way, when they wear Raquel's T-shirts.

So many people miss the opportunity to learn from their mistakes. It's in our failures and mistakes that we learn the most, and Raquel offers a beautiful example of how to embrace the messages that can arise from darker or unexpected moments.

We love hearing a mother of three boys talk about the importance of being feminine, staying true to yourself, and allowing your voice to lead others. Raquel is a shining example to all of us on how we can let go of stereotypes and other people's ideals so we can claim our own personality, strengths, and traits. This is one message we wish we could shout out from the rooftops for all young girls and grown women alike:

"There's nothing wrong with you. I designed you just as you are. Embrace it, live it, and bless others with it."

It's a fabulous way to redefine success and pave the way for others to do the same.

Chapter Challenge

What part of Raquel's story could you relate to the most?

_____

_____

If you could name only one thing you took away from this story, what would it be?

_____

_____

_____

What one thing will you do differently because of Raquel's story?

_____

_____

What surprised you the most in this story?

_____

_____

_____

If there was one thing you could ask Raquel, what would it be?

_____

_____

We'd love for you to connect with Raquel. If you'd like to connect with her, simply send an email to info@redefiningsuccessstories.com and put Raquel's name in the subject line

SHEDDING EXPECTATIONS

Neepa Sikdar

We only get one shot at this life and sometimes that means we have to ruffle some feathers along the way.

I sat crying in the bathroom stall. I could have picked a different bathroom to hide in, but the subway tile floors and enormous windows made this one my favorite. It was spotless and there was a separate section with full-length mirrors where the girls in my office would congregate on Thursday afternoons before happy hour. As I sat on the toilet with tears streaming down my face, I told myself to just breathe. My chest was pounding and tight, and my insides were swelling up like a balloon. "How did I get here?" I wondered. "How did I let this place take away my identity? How am I doubting myself and feeling inadequate?" People were always saying how lucky I was to have a job that most girls dream of. But it didn't feel that way to me. I often stayed at work until midnight, I'd come in on weekends and spent very little time with my family.

Realizing that I couldn't sit in that bathroom stall forever, I decided to get up and find B. I wiped my face, put on some makeup, and sent B an email to meet me at our spot, an accessories closet where we met to vent about the latest crazy work situation. I met her and told her my bathroom story and she said she could help; I just needed to give her ten minutes. I went back to my desk and a few minutes later she walked by and dropped off an envelope that read, "Open at home." Of course I couldn't wait that long, so I peeked inside to find a white pill with the word "Xanax" printed on top.

This was my answer. This was going to make everything better. The next 24 hours felt like a trip to Willy Wonka's Chocolate Factory. Popping anxiety pills like candy was a far cry from the dutiful daughter and woman I was supposed to be, and it wasn't the direction that I wanted to go. I ended up leaving that job and eventually the corporate world. But more on that later, first let me explain how I got there.

My life has been a series of steps that I was supposed to take, a list of unwritten rules that I was required to follow. My parents expected me to be a straight-A student, become a doctor, and marry a man from the right family. The culture I grew up in emphasized the importance of family and society over an individual's desires. And at every major milestone, I've trampled over these rules. My parents, being the remarkable people they are, haven't always understood my decisions, but they've always supported me. They've allowed me to make decisions, and encouraged me to form my own opinions. To understand my story, it's important to understand that my identity is deeply tied to my culture.

My family comes from East Bengal, an area that became East Pakistan after the British left India. My family is Hindu, making them a religious minority in a region dominated by Muslims. My father, an exceptional student, was denied admission to several universities due to his religion, until he was finally admitted to the one school that upheld a fair admission policy. This discrimination followed my dad into the workforce after graduation. Despite having friends who held high-level positions, he was denied promotions and job opportunities. To make matters worse, Pakistan considered Hindus spies for India and didn't allow them to have passports.

Eventually East Bengal fought for its independence from Pakistan and won. During the Bangladesh Liberation War of 1971, Bengalis suffered atrocities resulting in the genocide of three million people. At the same time, the United States was allowing entry of doctors, engineers and scientists from foreign countries to combat what they considered a "brain drain" in these fields, so my father applied for a visa. When I was five, my parents made the difficult decision to migrate to America, leaving behind family and friends. Their hope was to raise their daughter in a country where she could be free.

I grew up in New Jersey and considered myself American first, but was raised to be very proud of my Bengali culture and heritage. It wasn't always easy because there was no Mindy Kaling or Beyoncé on magazine covers or even Dora the Explorer on TV that I could identify with. My parents were insistent that I never forget my culture so we spoke our mother tongue, Bangla, at home and I spent weekends taking dance and writing classes. I'm proud to be a South Asian American, but it was difficult for me to be what the Bengali-American society wanted me to be. As I struggled between being a South Asian woman and an American woman, I actively chose to march to the beat of my own drum.

For starters, I didn't fit the stereotypical South Asian profile. I didn't major in science, IT, or engineering. I was one of the few people in my family who didn't have a master's degree, and not because I wasn't a good student; I got straight A's and joined various organizations in school. I was, and still am, an overachiever. Maybe this is because my culture instills a love of learning and being number one in academics. I decided if was going to march to the beat of my own drum, it sure as hell was going to be an awesome beat.

I had friends whose parents arranged their marriages by only allowing them to date their friends' kids. My parents had a "love marriage," not an arranged marriage, and they told me I would have the freedom to choose my husband. I was happy that my parents were open, especially when I saw my husband for the first time. I laid eyes on him and my heart skipped a beat. He was so handsome, he was well spoken and different from anyone I had met before. We fell deeply in love and marriage seemed inevitable.

But there was an enormous problem. He was Muslim. My parents left Bangladesh because of religious discrimination from Muslims and I here I was, in love with a Muslim man.

Friends and family demanded my parents stop the marriage. They were worried I would hurt their children's' future marriage proposals when potential suitors discovered what I had done. Many of my extended family members and several of my parents' friends didn't attend my wedding and a few even severed all ties with us because they objected so strongly. My husband's side was more supportive, but his parents lost friends when we got married too. I fell into a deep depression, tempered only by the amazing love I felt for my fiancé.

A girl's wedding day is supposed to be the happiest day of her life, yet mine was filled with anxiety and stress. I understood the objections were because people fear change, and I'm so grateful that my family displayed love through such a difficult time. Being American, I refused to believe I was committing a crime. I chose to marry a wonderful man who spoke the same language as my parents, who shared many of the same values and beliefs that I did, and most importantly, he loved me dearly. Almost 11 years later, this Bollywood romance has a happy ending as my wonderful husband has become well-accepted. Some of the original naysayers now tell my parents how lucky they are to have such a great son-in-law.

And while my happy marriage was beginning, my career was taking off. This was yet another life decision where I broke the status quo. As a girl, I was always experimenting with my personal style. My mom loved to dress me in girly pink dresses yet I absolutely despised them. I preferred striped dresses with matching blazers, belted pants, and dress shirts. I loved corduroys and colored jeans. I remember matching my Keds to my colored jeans in the early '90s when it was so trendy to mix colorful patterns with solids. I remember a beautiful white leather Liz Claiborne wallet with a silver buckle that my mom gave me. I took that wallet everywhere with me. It was the 1980s and Ms. Claiborne was a huge designer. I never imagined that I would end up working at the corporate offices of Liz Claiborne 20 years later. Those early days of fashion exploration taught me the importance of staying curious and to continually experiment with

28

my personal style.

In tenth grade, I was involved in my school's marketing organization, DECA, and co-managed our school store. Senior year I became president of the store, and I loved it. It lit a fire that I snuffed out as I convinced myself that a career in finance would be stable and lucrative. I spent two years working in corporate finance at a large private nuclear services company after college graduation and I hated it. I was bored to tears and there was no connection to a product I could touch and feel. I did some serious soul searching and read the famous book *What Color Is Your Parachute?* My real desire to work in merchandising as a fashion buyer started to break through.

I quit my job and moved to the epicenter of fashion, New York City. I remember my father saying, "Merchandising? What is merchandising? You could make more money in finance. Never quit a job until you have another one!" Once again, my family didn't understand my choice but they supported me anyway. I knew the only way to succeed would be to give it 100%. Landing a job in merchandising was tougher than I'd imagined. Temp agencies and recruiters discouraged me from the fashion world because I had no experience or family connections to open doors. The entry-level jobs paid peanuts and were reserved for those whose families could supplement their income. Hiring managers ignored my sales jobs at GAP and Target, and instead focused on the fact that I wasn't wearing head-to-toe designer labels. It was an uphill battle, but I was determined, and once I make a decision, nothing and no one can stop me.

Eventually I landed a two-week freelance assignment at J.Crew. It turned into a four-year permanent position. I hustled every single minute. I made a lot of mistakes but I also learned, and learned quickly. I learned about the real world: Life is not always fair and working hard does not always mean we'll be rewarded. I learned the art of the hustle. I learned how to do the most mundane, tedious task quickly and accurately. I learned not to work hard, but to work smart. I focused on the tasks that would make my business profitable instead of worrying about completing a never-ending to-do list. I learned about fabrics, quality, and garment construction from Jenna Lyons and J.Crew's design and production team. I met with Italian shoemakers who explained the entire process of creating a shoe and why certain handbags cost the same as a car. At any given moment our CEO would call our department to his office, which forced me to always be prepared and think on my feet. Building a defense for why I bought units of a certain style was better than any debate class I ever took. He also taught us about good customer service: to provide it and to demand it if it was denied.

At one point, I was asked to choose a style for our catalog cover.

Each page of the catalog had to be profitable, but the cover was reserved for items that were guaranteed to make six to seven figures. Our jewelry collection had recently launched and I chose a beautiful tiered necklace, called the Bubble Necklace. At $150, it was our most expensive jewelry item and I felt strongly about its potential. My planner was nervous that we didn't have enough units in stock. I said, "Go buy as much as you can and find out the earliest reorder date. This is going to be successful." My boss backed me and we fought to get it on the cover. We succeeded. That necklace became the number one style that month, for the *entire* company. We redeveloped in a variety of colors and it was featured in numerous fashion magazines and editorials. In the end, it became so popular that it had its own knock-offs.

After my four years at J.Crew, I moved to Liz Claiborne where I learned about the importance of mentors. My managers were not only great teachers, they went to bat for me and they became close friends. During my time at Liz, I would interact with Tim Gunn and John Bartlett. John Bartlett, a two-time CFDA (Council of Fashion Designers America) winner, was incredibly kind, immensely talented and taught me about men's apparel. But one of my favorite memories is of Tim Gunn. He was walking through the showroom with John Bartlett, and the outfits I had created for my presentation to department store buyers were hanging up. Tim stopped in front of

31

my looks and studied them before uttering his famous, "Good job. Make it work, people." I thought I'd died and gone to fashion heaven.

At this point in my career, I had gone from zero experience to managing a $40-million business in apparel and accessories. I had worked in wholesale (Liz Claiborne), retail stores (DKNY), ecommerce (J.Crew) and had experience in every category of men's and women's apparel and accessories. My experience made me a sought-after expert in the areas of handbags, footwear, and jewelry. In 2012, LinkedIn named me one of their top 2% most viewed profiles of the year, when they had approximately 250 million users. I was getting interviews all the time and I always made it to the final round. I interviewed at Oscar De La Renta, Barneys, Louis Vuitton Moet Hennessy, GAP, Banana Republic, Ann Taylor, Diesel, and DeBeers, to name a few.

So how did a woman with such a successful career end up crying in a bathroom stall at work? I had no balance in my life. I worked long hours and didn't spend enough time with my husband and daughter. I had high blood pressure and stress-induced migraines. Fashion is not the glamorous industry people think it is. It's full of hard people in high-level positions that prey on those with less power. It's also full of brilliant, kind, and talented individuals who tend to burn out and leave the industry. I had a choice to make, I could continue on this destructive unhealthy path and start popping pills or break free from that stall.

During this time, my cousin died suddenly at the age of 31. He was the closest thing I had to a brother growing up and I was devastated. Mired in grief and confusion, I began to question my faith in God. I needed a break, so I broke out of that stall and took one. I focused my time and energy on my daughter, my marriage, and myself. I sought out inspiration by traveling to Paris, London, and the Caribbean. I renewed my imagination at Disney World. Out of sheer luck, I got tickets to one of the final Oprah Winfrey tapings. The outfit I wore to the show got me a premium seat in the second row of the audience directly behind Ms. O. I was in the background of the entire episode. That day something magical happened: I felt a world of possibilities open up to me. I came home from Chicago renewed and determined to figure out my next steps. I went back to the drawing board. I desperately wanted something that would allow me to be creative, but also give me the freedom to set my hours and spend ample time with my family.

Even though the entrepreneurial juices were flowing I got scared. I took a job that was completely the wrong fit out of fear of not having stable income. My boss was a *Devil Wears Prada* type who took great pleasure in humiliating me. The day I quit that job, I went out to dinner with friends who encouraged me to finally start my personal styling business. I found the courage to go for it and I hired a new business mentor, Michelle Rodriguez. She and her Paid Stylist team helped me launch my company, Accessible Style.

Being a personal stylist is my dream job. My friends have always come to me for fashion advice, and I've loved boosting their confidence. It's not just about the clothes, it's the way you feel when you're wearing the right clothes. It's about clearing your mind of the self-limiting beliefs and negative internal dialogue. When we're young, we experiment, we're curious, and we're open to new things. Along the way we lose that curiosity and our personal style gets lost. Style evolves with every year of our lives through our adventures, and memories are contained in our wardrobe.

Every day is different and I feel a sense of exhilaration watching my clients transform their wardrobes and when they text me about how much they love their new looks and all the compliments they've received. There are good days and bad days and it's a lot of work. Balance is still a struggle but I'm so happy. I have the job that I've always dreamed of, because I created it. I'm a trendsetter, whether in my personal or professional life. I still march to the beat of my own drum, and you can bet that it's one stylish looking drum.

A note from Sarah and Ally: *We love that Neepa's story starts with her crying in the bathroom stall at work. How many of us have* *experienced that? We may not want to admit it, but so many times when we start pushing up against our own inner compass, things start to feel out of control and we know we're on the wrong path. When Neepa started sharing her story, we knew this was the perfect place to begin.*

Many of us have had moments like the one Neepa describes, when we know that it's time to make a change, or go with the crowd. There are times when we can feel lost or confused because what everyone else wants us to do doesn't work for us. The usual questions can come up, "Is there something wrong with me?" or "Why can't I just be like everyone else?" The first time we read through Neepa's story, we could imagine her struggle between popping pills or being true to herself. How many of our sisters have chosen to pop the pills? And how did we let it get like this? Just to work? We're all hoping this story reaches all the women out there who are facing these same questions.

Neepa has such a strong sense of self and inner strength. There is so much to learn from her tenacity starting out in the fashion world, and through her choice in husband: Nothing stops Neepa from stating what she wants and standing up for it, and in some cases, even losing family over it.

But what we love most about Neepa is that she is one of the warmest, kindest, and gentlest people you'll meet. She has a talent for turning the tide to her favor, and doing so with a smile and warmth. She makes friends as she moves along her path, gently bending all that's in her way to her will. A rare and truly successful combination.

Chapter Challenge

What part of Neepa's story could you relate to the most?

_____

_____

If you could name only one thing you took away from this story, what would it be?

_____

_____

_____

What one thing will you do differently because of Neepa's story?

_____

_____

What surprised you the most in this story?

_____

_____

_____

If there was one thing you could ask Neepa, what would it be?

_____

_____

We'd love for you to connect with Neepa. If you'd like to connect with her, simply send an email to info@redefiningsuccessstories.com and put Neepa's name in the subject line

RULE NUMBER ONE: KINDNESS

Sossie Dadoyan Arlia

No matter where we're from or what we've seen, we always have the power to spread kindness and warmth.

"Sossie is an unusual name. Where are you from?" is invariably the first question asked when I meet someone new. My name is Sossie Arlia, nee Dadoyan. I love my name, but I wanted to blend in and avoid talking about my ethnicity with every new encounter, so I started introducing myself as Sue.

I was born in Beirut in the beautiful country of Lebanon. I had a wonderful childhood, a loving family, and was surrounded by aunts and uncles, cousins, friendly neighbors, and had a busy social life. I have two older sisters and one younger brother. Our paternal grandma lived with us and I grew up listening to her telling us

39

fairytales and helping us with homework. After school, we walked home with friends or siblings, had a snack, and waited to hear our maternal grandpa's walking stick banging gently on our front door. He could hardly see and he would ask us to read the Armenian newspaper out loud to him. We took turns reading what we considered boring stuff, but we knew more about the Vietnam War than anyone else.

My dad was the owner of an import and export company. He worked long hours at his office, traveled for business, and spoke seven languages. In the summer months, when his secretary was on vacation, my sisters and I would work in his office. He made sure we didn't sit idle talking on the phone or filing our nails. He showed us how to type with the correct positioning of the fingers on the keyboard and he expected us to practice. I'm thankful he pushed us. My mom was the perfect housewife; going to the market every morning, buying fresh ingredients, and cooking meals from scratch for seven people. Mom was always happy and she sang while cooking in the kitchen. Later on, she started her own little business importing European dresses and selling them to family, friends, and neighbors. We were so proud of her!

My parents had a busy life, entertaining a lot, especially during Christmas and Easter. My maternal grandparents and all my relatives lived within a five-minute walking distance and we all visited each other without a phone call or appointment. Our church and my school were five minutes away from our house, as well as the sporting club where my siblings and I were signed up as scouts. The whole family was involved with different volunteer organizations: the Armenian Relief Society, cultural associations, amateur theatrical groups, chorus, folkloric dancing, and sports.

When I was four years old, I asked my grandma, "Grandma, why are a lot of Arab people living in our country?" She replied, "Sweetheart, this is an Arab country. It's their country. They allowed the Armenians to come and settle here." I was puzzled, but I let it go for the moment. I never forgot it because I could tell there was more to the story and I found it unsettling. I learned later about the Armenian Genocide of 1915 in Turkey. My paternal grandpa and all the men of the Dadoyan clan had been killed. By sheer luck, my grandma and her four young sons survived. My grandma raised her sons by herself, and they grew up to be honest, hard-working young men instilling the same values within their own families. Lebanon was our host country, and although I was Lebanese, I was brought up believing that one day, when the small country called Armenia was no longer occupied by the Soviet Union, we would all go back to our homeland.

The private Armenian school we attended followed the French educational model, which meant that kindergarten was made up of three classrooms for ages four, five, and six. It was located within the main school, but fenced in with a separate entrance and had a small covered playground. It had a little garden area to allow the children to plant in the spring. Every Friday, the teachers performed a puppet show, and we loved it. Our teachers offered the best in early childhood education and other teachers from all over Lebanon visited our kindergarten for training and learning.

Before entering first grade, we could read and write in both Armenian and French. In first grade, we were introduced to Arabic. By fifth grade, English classes started. Being exposed to American TV programs, movies, and music on the radio, we felt familiar with English. My classmates and I didn't take learning our fourth language very seriously, because all the state exams were in French. Had we known some of us would leave Lebanon and end up in the United States, we would have paid a little more attention during those English lessons.

The inscription under my high school yearbook photo says, "My wish for a future career working with children." During my free periods, I had started volunteering and helping out in the kindergarten classrooms and I loved it. I graduated high school and finished my freshman year of college. I picked French Literature as my major. I'd read all the French classics and I was certain I could get a job as a teacher or switch to journalism.

The summer before my second year of college, I got a job in a bank from 8:00 a.m. to 2:00 p.m. I didn't ask for this job, my father had heard about the availability of this position and volunteered me for it. I worked in the mornings and attended college in the afternoon. I never thought I'd work in a bank. Numbers and I weren't interested in each other. But as a good girl, I followed my father's wishes and entered the world of banking. I learned about the true meaning of the words "debit" and "credit" which helped me later on when I moved to the United States. I learned to work with colleagues, how to listen to my boss, the importance of confidentiality, and general business skills. I found it a bit of a shock to lose the lazy summer days at the beach or the pool with siblings and friends, and going to the movies any time we wanted. I had become a working girl, and at that age, not working seemed like a better option, especially in the summer!

It was during this time that I got married. My new husband and I were out almost every night with friends, carelessly lingering in restaurants and cafes in the beautiful city. With the help of our parents, we furnished our apartment, a small but adorable one. We weren't rich, but what we had was enough. Then the political events and civil war came to Lebanon in 1974 and changed the course of our lives. Our beautiful country was being destroyed, and we didn't understand why.

Muslims and Christians had been living in the same neighborhoods and had no problems with each other. There was no tension between religious or ethnic groups. Then overnight the city had a Muslim side and Christian side. My parents were now on the Muslim side, my sister and I were on the Christian side. Anyone trying to cross sides risked being shot by snipers. At night I could hear the sound of the bombs traveling from one side of the city to the other. One bomb landed on my parents' building and ricocheted across the street and killed our neighbor. A co-worker from the bank tried to cross the city, but was stopped by gunmen, robbed, and shot. I was petrified when a bomb fell a few buildings away from my apartment. I've never jumped so high in my life, instinctively seeking safety. I can still hear the sound in my ears. I was so upset that my husband decided to take me away to his parents' house. I missed my parents, I could only call them if the phones were working, but I wanted to be with them. We decided to take long detours to get to their summer house. The 25-minute drive took us three hours, and we weren't even sure if the roads were open or accessible. We were stopped several times by gunmen who asked us where we were headed and why. Finally we made it safely, and I got to see my parents. But we had to keep moving. We stayed in 11 different places in two years.

I lost friends and I witnessed bodies being dragged in the streets. The universities and schools were damaged from the bombs and many simply shut down. A whole generation of children missed years of school, until arrangements were made to transfer whole schools, including mine, to the mountains. The downtown area was totally destroyed. My father's office was gone. He never worked in it again. Slowly people started leaving. The Lebanon that I had known and loved was gone. Even the most optimistic among us saw no end in sight.

For a while, we hoped there would be a resolution. But the war got worse and we decided to sell everything and move out of Lebanon. Our destination was France where my middle sister, her husband, and their infant daughter had moved a few months earlier. Before she left, she made me promise that I would follow her as soon as I could, saying, "I don't want to leave without you. I want our family to be together." But by the time we were ready to leave, the airport was shut down, so we had no other choice than to book a travel pass on a yacht that took us to Cyprus. We stayed in Cyprus for a few days and then left for Paris. My husband and I both got jobs and settled into a new routine. We loved France but financially it was hard to make ends meet. We really wanted to come to the United States. My older sister was in California and my husband's sister was in Boston. She was engaged at the time and when we received the invitation to her wedding, we decided to leave Paris. In January 1977 we arrived in the United States and moved to New Jersey after her wedding. We found sponsors and finalized our green card applications through a program in our church. We became proud American citizens a few years later.

The best thing that ever happened to me was the birth of my son Mark in November 1977. I'd miscarried in France and it left me traumatized. I was afraid I would never have children so the birth of my son was a time of pure love and joy. We lived on my husband's small salary, but with careful planning we made it work. My mom was still in Beirut because her parents were old and she was taking care of them. My brother was in Paris, my older sister was in Los Angeles, and my middle sister had followed me and settled in Boston.

When my son was around one year old, my middle sister and her family moved to New Jersey. We were finally together! She started working in a bridal store in the mall while I watched her two children. When I was ready to work, we switched, and she took care of my son. My only experience at that time was working in a bank so I applied at one and got hired. I couldn't believe my good fortune! I liked going to work. The pay was minimum wage, but I didn't care. The only thing that I didn't like about this huge bank was the way the employees were treated. They had strict rules including no personal phone calls. When my son was sick, I couldn't use the phone to see how he was doing. After two years, I applied to another bank, and got a better position with a slightly higher salary. The atmosphere in this bank was much better and I took note of how differently the employees were treated. Going to work now was fun.

When some friends mentioned that a nursery school was for sale in a nearby town and they suggested I buy it and run the school, I figured they were crazy, but on second thought, there was no harm in visiting. When I saw the school, I could see myself working with these amazing children and I fell in love with the idea. We borrowed money for the down payment from our church, friends, and parents. We applied for a second loan on our house and *voila*! We had the down payment and I became the proud owner of Jack in the Box School, Inc., in Closter, New Jersey. It was one of the first nursery schools in our county and it had been in operation for decades when I became the owner. I'd never been a boss and I was determined to earn the respect of parents and co-workers. There was a great deal for me to learn.

After resigning from the bank, I spent a few hours every day at the Jack in the Box School where the previous owner showed me how to run the school. After the closing, I embarked on my new path with butterflies in my stomach. I was happy and grateful for the opportunity, but I had fears of failing or saying or doing the wrong thing. When I was expressing my fears to a friend who has been successful in business, he said, "Just follow your gut feelings and you'll be fine." This was important advice, and whenever I haven't listen to my inner voice, I've regretted it.

Jack in the Box Early Learning Center is in a small house that was converted into a school. The décor in the school was mostly brown: brown wall paneling, brown wall-to-wall carpet and windows that were closed off to keep heat in. As I was feeling more comfortable with running the school, whenever I had extra money, I would start a renovation project. I could see how it would look if I removed the walls and changed the position of the doors to make everything flow nicely and utilize the space better. In my 32 years at the school, the fire alarm system has been replaced three times. I reopened the windows that were closed off and upgraded the electricity. Instead of covering the electric outlets with plastic covers, I asked the electrician to move them up higher so that the children couldn't reach them. During inspection visits, we get compliments on the cleanliness of the school, the impeccable paperwork, and the excellent child to teacher ratio.

In 2000, we were running at full capacity and we had a waiting list. We heard that there was a classroom available for rent five minutes away from our school in a town called Alpine. I consulted with Miss Christine, my co-director, and she agreed to work in Alpine and that September, we opened our second school! Then in 2007, we received a phone call from a church in a neighboring town, Tenafly, informing us that their nursery school was closing and they offered us the space to rent. I knew our working parents wanted a place for their newborns, so I said yes. I needed an experienced director to run it. I turned to Miss Christine again, and she took on the challenge. I signed the contract in April, and started planning the renovations. In July and August, I was in Tenafly every day, designing the infant room, hiring local artists to paint and draw beautiful pictures on some of the walls. The place was swarming with carpenters and electricians. This was a major beautification project. In August, Miss Christine started working in Tenafly. She trained the teachers and showed the school to prospective parents. We opened the school in September with five classrooms filled with adorable children and babies!

I wasn't taught how to be a boss, but I created rule number one: kindness. All new staff members know about rule number one. I respected their education, but kindness towards children, colleagues, and parents is a must.

When I was asked to be part of this book, my first thought was, "They have the wrong woman. I haven't created an empire or made millions of dollars. I'm the owner of a small business." Then I reminded myself that success isn't just about money, it's about the ups and downs of life and being brave despite the obstacles we all face. In 1989 I got divorced and went through a couple of

49

emotionally taxing years. Being divorced is something you don't get used to, but as the saying goes, time heals all wounds. I met and married my second husband, and we both love to travel, which we do as often as our schedules permit.

I am proud that I have helped some young_parents who couldn't afford our tuition. We've mentored young teachers, a process that requires mountains of paperwork and countless hours. When their certifications are approved, we encourage these young teachers to move on and find high-paying positions in public schools. Over the last five years, we've held fundraisers, and the wonderful parents from my schools have donated $16,000 to various children's health organizations.

None of us find success on our own. I'm grateful to my sister and my late mom who watched my son while I worked long hours at the school and sometimes on weekends. My son got married in 2009 to a beautiful young lady whom I love as a daughter. Now that I'm a grandma, my grandchildren attend my schools. I'm grateful to all the wonderful teachers and directors that I work with. I couldn't have done it without them. I'm grateful to be an American, and I'm happy that I took advantage of all the opportunities this wonderful country offers. I'm grateful to my parents for instilling in me a love of volunteering and supporting the community. That love has led me to sit on many non-profit organizations, including as a director on the board of the Closter Chamber of Commerce, and being on the board of a non-profit nursery school in a less affluent area.

I'm glad I said yes to the adventure that put me on this path 32 years ago. It's been wonderful for my family and me and my life is rich with an abundance of friends, parents, and co-workers. I love my job because I am greeted every morning by the smiling faces of the children. It pleases me to no end to see an alumna working at our school because she loved our preschool so much, and her dream of teaching at Jack in the Box School is now a reality.

Was I a little foolish to jump into owning a business without experience? Maybe. But it's worked out very well. When you love what you do, it always does.

A note from Sarah and Ally: It's amazing what women can do when we put our minds to it, isn't it? All through Sossie's story, the picture of her beautiful Lebanon left a lasting impression. What's it like as a young newlywed in college, watching your beloved city be torn apart by war? Or to worry if you'll ever see your own sister again or that you'll be killed for walking across the street? Many times we hear that we don't know what we're truly capable of handling until we're in the middle of a crisis, but even with that in mind, I don't know how many of us could pick up after watching that kind of destruction.

The hope that Sossie's story brings is so important for all of us to remember. Not only did she pick up after seeing war and terror, she moved to a new country and then trusted herself enough to borrow from family, friends, and banks to make a lifelong dream come true. Out of the chaos that started her life, she's created a sanctuary for small children, passing on a sense of hope, peace, and beauty.

There is a little bit of magic in Sossie's story, and an awful lot of hard work. Her journey illustrates what's possible when we put our minds to something, and then do the work that's needed to bring it to fruition. We can surely rely upon the powers that be, whatever those powers are for each of us personally, but we can't rely upon them while we sit at home on the couch. It takes work, creativity, and passion – all of which Sossie has in spades. Whenever any of us think we have it "hard" or that outward circumstances could break us, we can think of Sossie and know that we too, can make magic wherever we are.

Chapter Challenge

What part of Sossie's story could you relate to the most?

_____

_____

If you could name only one thing you took away from this story, what would it be?

_____

_____

_____

What one thing will you do differently because of Sossie's story?

_____

_____

What surprised you the most in this story?

_____

_____

_____

If there was one thing you could ask Sossie, what would it be?

_____

_____

We'd love for you to connect with Sossie. If you'd like to connect with her, simply send an email to info@redefiningsuccessstories.com and put Sossie's name in the subject line.

THE TIME TO BE HAPPY IS NOW

Jennifer Dawn

Life will rarely deliver the perfect circumstances to us, so it's our job to make the most of what we're given and use the present moment to push ourselves forward.

I was born in the tiny desert town of Kingman, Arizona, which is known for nothing. Never having met my biological father and having been sexually molested by the one who called himself Daddy, I learned from an early age to meet the needs of others or bad things would happen.

My parents' marriage was a battleground of religion, infidelity, dirty secrets, and money troubles. By seventh grade I had been in 13 different schools. We were not a military family, just screwed up. I'll never forget the day I sat down and counted up how many

55

schools I had been in. I'd stopped trying to make friends because it was pointless.

The sexual abuse started when I was four. Or at least that's the earliest I'm willing to remember. I stood in the kitchen one day and told my mom that daddy kept getting into the shower with me. A fight ensued where he clearly stated, in front of me, that I was a liar. My mom believed him. That's the day I learned I was alone in this world and nobody was going to protect me. The abuse went on for years and one day in high school I realized that my dad was not like the other dads. He never once looked at me like a daughter. He looked at me like an object when I was younger, and like a *woman* as I'd grown up.

I survived by playing the role of "good daughter." Early on I decided that other people's behavior, no matter how horrific, would *not* define my life. I was determined to rise above it no matter what and that's what I did. Years later, while in therapy, I learned that this was a coping mechanism. A damn good one, if you ask me.

My mother's parents were my saving grace. Each summer my sisters and I were dropped off in Kingman and we got to stay there, without my parents, for three whole months. Every morning kids and dogs piled in an old Chevy pickup and my grandfather drove us out to the horses. I spent the morning tearing across the desert on my little pony

Shadow or on the big sorrel mare, Cinnamon. Then, we all came home and jumped into the pool to cool off as grandma made us breakfast from scratch.

My grandfather was a chiropractor and worked from an office attached to the house. I guess this model stuck with me because I'm most happy when working from my own home, like I do today. I was the first grandchild and the favorite. It wasn't some secret the adults shared among themselves. It was well known and I can't imagine how it must have felt for my three younger sisters trying to compare. Being the favorite and "perfect" I had to live up to the title. Striving for perfection followed me well into adulthood until I finally figured out that the idea of perfection is bullshit and an impossible standard to maintain if you ever want to be truly happy.

I followed my grandfather around like a shadow. When he went out to the garden to pick a few ears of corn or pluck some tomatoes off the vine I was right beside him. When he went back into the office to see a patient, I was at the front desk greeting folks, making appointments, and filling out patient charts.

I started working full-time over the summers in his office when I was only ten. My grandmother said she couldn't find an adult who did the job better than I did. I was making five bucks an hour, buying all my own school clothes, and thought I was pretty hot stuff. I had a natural affinity for business, loved working with people, and to me it didn't feel like work at all. I was never expected to work, but I really enjoyed it. The concept of trading time and talent for money was easy for me to embrace.

Those peaceful Arizona summers ended when I was 12. There was a lot of "adult" stuff going on I didn't understand but what I did know was that one day my grandmother asked me about my father and what he had been doing to me. I saw no reason to lie to her, so I told the truth. That's when the shit hit the fan. A war broke out between my grandparents and parents. My mother pretended not to know what had been going on and chose to "stand by her man." A few months later our family moved over 2,000 miles east and landed in Panama City, Florida.

It was an armpit. It stunk and I hated it. I had loved my last school and felt so out of place in Florida. It was the first time I ever missed the bus on purpose because I despised the school so much. I went from the desert to the ocean; from having friends to none; from a big house with my own room to a tiny crap hole and sharing with my sisters; from seeing my grandparents to losing them completely. And to make matters worse, I felt like it was my fault. If I'd lied to my grandmother maybe none of it would have happened.

After a year in Panama City we moved again. This time I welcomed the move. My dad bought some 200-year-old house at a local auction for $10,000 and we moved in. You could see the ground below through the holes in the floorboards, but the new school was much better and I finished my eighth grade year feeling less out of place. Then, I started high school and for the first time ever, we stayed in the same place for four years.

I recently looked up my high school on Great Schools and it was rated a two out of ten. Back then, the rating system didn't exist and frankly I didn't care. I loved it. I was on the honor roll, I was a cheerleader, I took stats for the football team, and later I became editor of the yearbook and president of the Kiwanis club. I worked hard and enjoyed every minute of it.

My freshman year I also became best friends with a petite brunette named Shannon. We both made the cheerleading team and we were inseparable. I'd spent my whole life without really close friends and this was something very special to me. We drank our first beer together, passed notes in class, and our boyfriends happened to be best friends too.

One afternoon as Shannon was driving home she slid through a stop sign and was T-boned by a speeding truck. I sat at her bedside with her mother and a few close friends later that night in the hospital. I watched that little line on the monitor go flat as her heart stopped beating. That day I learned just how precious real friendship is.

Even though I was no longer allowed to work for my grandparents, that doesn't mean I stopped working. I started my own cake decorating business in high school and worked as a word processor in the local print shop. I graduated high school when I was 17, left home that summer, and never looked back. I quickly landed a job with the State of Florida and eventually went to work as a graphic designer in the governor's office. As I was growing up, the only thing my family ever said about college was, "We're not paying for it." So while I worked full-time during the day I put myself through classes at night.

I was 19 when the call came that my grandfather had passed away. My parents weren't going to the funeral. "Too expensive" to make the trip, they said. But, this was my grandfather, the man who'd meant everything to me. So I took what I had in savings, maxed out my credit cards, rented a minivan, and drove my family to Arizona for the funeral. I wiped myself out financially, but it was worth it. My parents said they would pay me back but that never happened. When I got back home I had to drop out of school and get a second job to keep the debt collectors at bay. I took a night post at a funeral home of all places.

During my time at the "home" I saw a four-year-old little boy who had drowned and looked like he was sleeping in the casket; a mother of four older children who had been stalked and then shot by her ex-husband while planting flowers in her front yard; and an elderly man who passed away and was followed by his wife a few months later when she took her own life.

It was sad as hell, but also the place where I laughed the most. The staff was amazing, lighthearted, and funny, always playing jokes on each other. We had to be like that or the reality of our work would be too much. I'll never forget the time one director climbed into a body bag and rolled into the back room to give the staff a little surprise. Or when the cremation room was being cleaned and the staff decided to fire up the engine just to see if the maintenance guy was paying attention. The funeral home taught me there was so much more to life than death. The big things that matter aren't money or possessions, but rather who you love and how much you're loved in return.

I went on to work for IBM and then a small company that sold point of sale systems to amusement parks. I was single, traveled all over the country, and I loved it. The part I didn't take to so well was the crappy software and bad customer service. That drove me nuts and I knew I could do better.

At 23, I stared my own company. It was just my fiancé at the time, and me. He was a software developer and I was everything else. I had no idea what I was doing, but I knew I wanted to create something remarkable. When I ran our first marketing advertisement I remember him asking me, "Why in the world are you doing that?" Some things you shouldn't have to explain. It was a sign of things to come.

The first year in business my total sales came to $300, and I worked my ass off round the clock. When I say I pulled "all-nighters," I mean it. I'd work for 36 or 48 hours straight to finish a big project. Not only did I design the software but I also sold it, installed it, trained the client on how to use it, provided ongoing support for it, and poured all the love I had into it. I took the company from nothing to over seven figures. I learned so much, mostly through trial and error, but without a doubt it was the stubborn determination all entrepreneurs share that always kept me going.

After ten years and two kids I was tired. My marriage had been struggling but I'd felt unable to make a change because my business and personal life were so tightly entwined. Late one evening, returning home after a 52-hour flight from Cairo, Egypt, I was utterly exhausted. As I pulled into the driveway, barely able to keep my eyes open, I realized my husband had parked right in the middle of the driveway. As if I didn't even exist. It was right then I realized that if I didn't make a change I would die. Not physically, but in my soul.

I was losing traction daily.

I had no idea how it would unfold but I resolved to take the first step. I hired movers, and eventually sold my shares of the company. That led me to accept a position with a large $54-million manufacturing firm as their software division president. I felt spoiled having my own marketing, accounting, and human resources department when I had been doing all that by myself for years.

At the time I was the only senior female executive in a totally male dominated industry. I had so much experience I could do the job in my sleep, but I wasn't passionate about the work. I grew their sales significantly but found the morals and decision making of the founder out of alignment with my own values. I also realized that the nanny knew my kids better than I did. The money was plentiful and steady but Corporate America was not where I belonged.

Leaving was scary, but I had my kids to think about and that was pretty good motivation. I started consulting and writing right away and picked up a client who was an intuitive energy healer. I truly love all that woo-woo stuff but when she told me I should immediately re-brand myself as a business coach and there was big money in it for me I'll admit to skepticism. I thought, "Why in the hell would I want to be a business coach?"

Instead I kept to the writing, met and married a truly wonderful man, and re-located to New York State. It was there I was retained by a women's networking organization to run their accountability and mastermind groups. I took to the work like bees to buttercups. Quite by accident, I found a passion for mentoring the women entrepreneurs in our network. My experience as a business owner and top female executive was extensive and I loved using my own hard-earned wisdom to shorten the path for others. Eighteen months later I began Jennifer Dawn Coaching and have been going strong ever since. I guess that psychic was right. Go figure.

Now, I get to hand-pick my clients, set my own hours, and work from home so I'm available to my family. I also get my hands around lots of different businesses, which is like candy to me. Is my life perfect? Hell no. Nothing in life ever is. But it is a life that is perfect for me and one I've worked hard to earn.

I used to fall into the trap of thinking: When my business makes a million dollars *then* I'll be happy. When I finally meet the right man, *then* I'll be happy. When I lose 10 pounds, *then* I'll be happy. And you know what? Waiting for something to happen before I could be happy was crap. My time to be happy is *now*.

That's not to say I don't have goals or challenge myself, or still need to lose 10 pounds. I still have bad days when the pain of my past is triggered and it takes all of me to come back. But I do love where I am, appreciate how I got here, and am grateful to have survived this far. I've found a real power and peace in acceptance.

What's next for me? I believe that how I spend my time today will affect where I am in one year, five years, or twenty years; every day matters. I have a horse of my own now, and I love riding him, I spend time on the back of the motorcycle with my hubby, and I'm consistently working to put more zeros at the end of the bank account. I'm still helping others, growing a business, and most importantly, still in control of my own happiness.

There is no gap between where I am today and where I want to be tomorrow. There are just experiences to live, lessons to learn, and fun to be had. I've learned to slow it down a bit and take each day for what it has to offer. Most importantly I want to look back and say, "Yep, I got every bit of juice sucked clean dry out of life's orange." My favorite inspirational quote is from Dolly Parton. She said, "You'll never do a whole lot unless you are brave enough to try." To me that's the first and most important step: try. If you don't do that you've lost the race before even getting out of the starting gate.

Today my biggest source of joy is my family. We are not traditional by any means but we are the real deal. Even when my teenager is complaining about something (anything), I'm so thankful to be around her and not stuck in some cubicle for ten hours a day. I love taking my son to Little League and the heart attack that comes each time I watch him steal a base. I get to be there every morning and afternoon to put my six-year-old on the bus. When I think she will get to attend the same school, in the same town, and grow up with the same friends for her entire childhood, it brings tears to my eyes. To give my children what I never had makes me feel like I've come full circle, and healed what was hurt.

Looking back now, sure there are things I wish never happened. But they did and I can't change them. These experiences have made me who I am. I'm happy because I choose to be. I know abuse, sadness, deceit, grief, and heartbreak well. But, they've also shaped me to be strong enough to choose what I really want in life and go after it. After a life of "surviving" one of the scariest feats has been learning to live in safety. What I want most is to be free and feel love and let the rest of the crap go. Of course the right husband and lots of therapy has also been a godsend.

The advice I have to offer is to follow your heart, do the work, and enjoy every moment. It's your life so no matter what you've been handed, you might as well make the most of it.

A note from Sarah and Ally: *As we shared just after Sossie's story, for women who are determined to make it, the circumstances we're born into can only affect us for so long before we break free of them and start finding our way. There are so many vivid pieces of Jennifer's story that stick with us; knowing that no one would be with her when she was young; losing her grandparents when she decided to be honest; realizing her husband didn't acknowledge her. There are always going to be opportunities for us to give up, and we'll always get to choose between backing down or shedding what doesn't work and moving forward.*

That being said, it's not always that easy. Leaving a marriage is incredibly difficult, even if it's one that doesn't fit anymore. Daring to tell the truth when you don't know what will happen can be terrifying. It takes great courage to continue to stand up when life delivers some serious right hooks.

But what's so impressive and memorable about Jennifer's story is that she didn't just stand up. She stood up, brushed herself off, learned how to laugh, and refused to believe in limits. This woman built and sold a multimillion-dollar company! That is so hard and takes so much work, dedication, and fortitude! It's like she was able to pull strength from the bad and literally turn it into gold. While the path to success can be winding, it's always ours, and Jennifer is a beautiful illustration of that idea.

She ends her story with the line, "You might as well make the most of it." And we find that to be quite humble. She does more than make the most of it, she's squeezed every last drop out of life and shown us all how to dance in the rain.

Chapter Challenge

What part of Jennifer's story could you relate to the most?

_____

_____

If you could name only one thing you took away from this story, what would it be?

_____

_____

_____

What one thing will you do differently because of Jennifer's story?

_____

_____

What surprised you the most in this story?

_____

_____

_____

If there was one thing you could ask Jennifer, what would it be?

_____

_____

We'd love for you to connect with Jennifer. If you'd like to connect with her, simply send an email to info@redefiningsuccessstories.com and put Jennifer's name in the subject line.

YOU MATTER

Sarah Walton

Life can dish out its worst and make you feel invisible, but you always have the choice to dig deep, find your voice, and create your own happiness.

My heart was pounding and my mouth was dry. I was in our small, cramped and dimly lit conference room where everything of importance in our tiny little startup happened. My stomach was in knots. I had that lightheaded rush that comes with adrenaline, and I was acutely aware that I was out of my element. I didn't ask for raises. I was a good girl. I did my job and was grateful for what I received in return. I didn't rock the boat like this.

But my boss, a young man who was far too good-looking for his own good, had just finished talking. In his usual smooth and nonchalant way, he had delicately let me know that my raise wasn't going to be as big as I had hoped, and that I should be fine with that. He didn't say it in quite those words, he was a charmer to be sure, and I knew he really liked me and appreciated my work. I was the second employee hired at this startup, and I was managing all of the day-to-day operations. He knew I was valuable. But more importantly, I knew that he knew.

In an out-of-body experience, something deep inside me kicked in, and I heard these words come out of my mouth, "Thank you. And no." And I slid the piece of paper he'd offered me back across the table.

He looked down for a moment, then back up and blinked several times, quite rapidly. I'm not sure if he was pleasantly surprised or shocked. This was a man who was used to getting his way in business, and with women. He knew business, and he certainly knew how to negotiate. I, on the other hand, at the ripe old age of 26, did not. Yet. In addition, we were both used to me doing what needed to be done, no matter the cost.

But over the last few months I'd realized how much I was worth, and how much I wasn't being paid. "Look," I said, "I'm not asking for anything unreasonable here. I'd like to eat out once in a while, and I don't know, maybe go to the movies. I can't do that on what you're paying me now, and I've earned this raise. Why don't you let me know what you can really do?" I stood up and walked out.

Let me pull you out of this scene and take you back to my childhood. Ah, the beautiful, albeit very dry, suburban delights of Sandy, Utah. I lived there with my mom and my younger half-brother. My parents got divorced when I was 18 months old, and I loved telling my friends that I'd be gone over the weekend, visiting my dad in Los Angeles. There were parts of my childhood that were absolutely idyllic. I remember playing Kick-the-Can in the street with our neighbors long after the sun went down. My best friend Katie had a tree in her front yard that we loved to climb up and spend hours playing card games, making up stories, and hiding behind the leaves as we spied upon unsuspecting neighbors and cute boys riding by on their bikes.

Then there were the *other* parts of childhood. As can happen in any family, I was being sexually abused by my uncle, my mother's youngest brother. I don't know exactly when the abuse started, but I don't remember a time when it wasn't happening. As children, whatever we're born into is "just the way it is." Until the day comes when we realize that it's not "just this way" for every child.

That day came for me when I was four years old, sitting in my grandmother's kitchen playing Frogger on Atari. My uncle came up behind me and slid his hands down the back of my pants. There was a pause, and then a siren went off inside my head. My heart started to race, and for the first time, I was startled and afraid. I froze in utter terror. My heart was pounding so hard I could feel its pressure in my eyes as I stared up at my grandmother's lime green and deep blue stained glass chandelier over the kitchen table. From somewhere outside myself, I heard a deep gasp and then the words, "I'm all alone!" I ended up carrying those words with me for most of my life, even as I've worked to dismantle them.

As children we cope and we move through our lives letting things go and focusing on the moment. The abuse stopped when I was around 11 years old, but that moment in the kitchen, the invisible aspects of the abuse, didn't stop so easily. Children who are abused understand very early on that we're being objectified. We certainly don't have the vocabulary to describe it, but we know. The message that comes through loud and clear is, "You're here to please me, and you don't matter." I was clear that my job was to please others, and that my needs didn't matter. This is why the scene in that dimly lit conference room was such an important one for me. I was learning to use the voice that had been silenced when I was four.

We have little control over the events that shape us when we're young, but as we age, we have the ability to look at those events, admit they happened, and then dictate the level of effect we'll allow them to have on us as we move forward. That, in my opinion, is where the real success lies. As a coping mechanism, I learned how to be the center of attention around my friends, and how to make people laugh. I learned how to deflect, please, and read the needs of other people. It's a skill I use almost daily and I'm sure it's contributed to my success.

When I was twelve, during one of my visits to LA, my dad and I were on our way to meet his new girlfriend, Deborah. I turned to him and said, "I hate meeting new people, Dad. She's going to ask me a million questions, and I don't want to talk about what I'm going to be when I grow up or what my favorite color is or deal with all that small talk." My dad thought for a minute before he spoke (a trait I did not inherit but greatly admire) and said, "Well, why don't you turn it around on her? You should ask *her* all those questions! It'll be funny, and *she's* funny!" He chuckled at his own brilliance and I thought, "That's right. You laugh at your own jokes while I sit through dinner and answer questions."

Turns out, Deborah just talked with me. She knew something about everything, and I remember sitting at the table at our favorite Thai restaurant, Siam Cottage in Century City, thinking, "Wow. She sure can talk," and I loved it. I didn't know that I was sharing chicken satay and veggie pad thai with a woman who would be instrumental in changing the course of my life. I've found that life often puts the perfect people in our path, right when we need them. But it's up to us to recognize them and accept the help that's offered.

Over the following years, Deborah would call me once a week and talk to me about college, boys, friends, and anything else under the sun. She pushed me to think outside of what I was seeing around me. I wasn't raised to think about college or what I wanted to do with my life; I was raised to think about marriage and babies. Little did I know, Deborah was intentionally, and methodically, introducing me to other ways of life. She introduced me to New York City, she noticed and encouraged my brains, and she worked diligently to get me out of the world I was in, and into the world that was waiting for me. I'm not sure how you thank someone for something like that, but I hope her step-grandkids are a good start.

I did move out of Utah eventually. I went to UCLA to be closer to Deborah and my dad and I graduated with honors. I loved living in LA, especially in January and February when I could wear sundresses to class and study by the rooftop pool of my apartment building. After graduation, I spent almost a year living in the south of France before returning to the States. I moved to the Big Apple armed with a suitcase and $200. I lived with a family friend and was very nervous about money. I hit the pavement of Manhattan and got my first job waiting tables within the first week. I had the pleasure of waiting on Jerry Seinfeld, a few soap opera stars, and many tipsy Wall Street interns on Thursday nights. I loved it, but after a few months, I knew it was time for me to start looking for a "real" job.

Like many young, ambitious women before me, I headed straight into a headhunter's office and handed over my skimpy résumé. I was ready to take on New York City and make my way in the world. I told the headhunter I'd like to work in an office and try my luck at marketing, or maybe fashion, or something. I had no idea, to be honest. But I did say, "Don't send me to a bank, and don't put me in a room by myself." So of course, she did both. I landed at Montgomery Prime Brokerage, which would soon become part of Bank of America, where I was a receptionist, in a room by myself. I passed the hours by reading the New York Times, and imagining myself as a famous writer, in high demand for my journalistic brilliance. I spent the rest of the time laughing with my co-workers, flirting with the young account executives, and making new friends.

One of those friends ended up helping me gain a whole new skill set that launched my career. Meena, the head of Montgomery's technical support division, strolled up to my desk one day, and asked me the fabulous question: "Aren't you bored sitting out here all day?" It was 1998, and the world was just starting to understand that websites were important. She took one discerning look at me, threw *HTML for Dummies* and *Photoshop for Dummies* on my desk, said nonchalantly, "Make me a website," and walked away. I devoured those books. I loved learning the code, playing with Photoshop, and launching case studies for the best location of buttons, logos, and links on a site. I made Meena a few websites, and she hired me.

I don't think the six men on Meena's team were thrilled to have me there, but I didn't care. I vividly remember signing my paperwork, selecting my 401k allocations, and receiving my health insurance coverage. I was so anxious to be on my own, to prove that I could be independent and successful and I was so proud walking down the hall with my folder full of information on the morning I became an employee. I was official. I'd found a job in New York City. My day-to-day consisted of answering technical support calls coming in from the hedge fund managers whose trade instruments weren't working properly. I was always the first one to answer the phone on the desk, and I worked hard to learn every detail of our technology. I learned how to set up new computers, create e-mail accounts on our exchange servers, and get yelled at with grace when the technology wasn't working.

Shortly after the Y2K scare, I knew that helping wealthy people make more money wasn't my calling. I turned to another headhunter who got me an interview at Lifetime Television with their New Media department. I instantly fell in love with the environment and the team and I was thrilled when offered the job at twice what I'd been making getting screamed at by hedge fund managers. I was there for four years, and I grew up in that office. While I was there, I moved in with my boyfriend, got engaged, planned a wedding and then called it off. I learned to keep secrets, work as a team, and the importance of watching other people before acting. I loved that job and it was thrilling to get to work on web pages that millions of people were viewing. Now my love of technology was used to help people sign breast cancer petitions, to entertain, and to launch vibrant discussions among women about topics that mattered.

After four years, the itch to push my limits and take on more responsibility turned into a burning rash. During a regular phone call with my close friend Lara, I said, "OK. I think I know what I want to do. I want to still build websites, but I want to work with someone like Marianne Williamson and do something that inspires other people." The next day, Lara ran into an old colleague she hadn't seen in years. They got to talking and it turns out Lara's friend had just been hired by my about-to-be boss to find someone exactly like me. That one conversation led me to the startup I wrote about earlier. They were looking for their second employee, someone who could help Marianne Williamson with her new digital project. When I heard that, I think my faith in the universe, or the "powers that be" was solidified. It was just too coincidental. I got the job, and several months later, after dedication, late hours, and non-stop working weekends, I found myself in that conference room, asking for a raise.

Two years later, after turning our little startup into a company with 18 employees, midtown offices, and paying customers, I met my husband, Andy. After a whirlwind 28 days, he proposed. The crazy part: I said yes. We eloped and were married nine weeks after the day we met. We've been married for ten years and have two amazing children. I went from a single woman and vice president at a startup, to a wife and working mother in under one year. Suddenly my career didn't seem so important. I never imagined anything could draw my attention away from work, but becoming a mother changed everything for me. For years after my children were born, I would swing back and forth between wanting to be a CEO and a stay-at-home-mom. Luckily for me, I've been able to create a combo, but only after six years of internal struggle, sleepless nights, and confusion.

The last corporate job I held was my favorite of all. I was the general manager for a division of Mindspark, an IAC company. I've made great friends at every job I've had, but there was something quite special about that specific team. At some point during that job, I knew I'd made it. I'd moved across the country and climbed to the top in the toughest city in the world. I was exhausted, and a lot of things weren't perfect, but I was making great money, I had an amazing team, I got to pitch directly to Barry Diller, the company's owner, I had a ficus tree in my office, and I spent my lunch hours at Nordstrom. I'd donate money through micro-loans for women in poorer nations so they could start their own companies, I brought in treats for my colleagues, I had great clothes, and I took my family to Disney World.

But these outward markers of success weren't working for me. I only saw my kids in their pajamas during the week. Our nanny was absolutely wonderful, but I hated not being home with my kids. After all of this ladder climbing, learning how to negotiate, ("Thank you. And no."), I'd put in all of this work to "make it," to find my voice, but now I wanted even more. I was completely baffled, and absolutely torn apart. I would wake up in the middle of the night terrified that I had missed a special moment with my kids, or that I'd forgotten something they needed for school. My husband is so great at those things, and he would always remember, but I hated that it wasn't me. I resented my husband's flexible schedule and I found every excuse to start a fight. Then my chest started hurting, almost constantly.

After much hemming and hawing, I made my exit from corporate America. It's been one hell of a ride since then. I've created different companies, had more ideas than I can count, and thrown some of those ideas out into the market to test them. The highlight of my entrepreneurial career was when one of my companies was featured on the *Today Show*. I remember getting the call that we'd been selected to appear as part of a segment on women who've reinvented themselves. Seeing my picture plastered all over national TV, and doing all the work to prepare for that broadcast was truly exciting. It was the moment when I knew that I could do anything I set my mind to. As long as I work hard and listen to my instincts, I have a great shot at success. When preparation meets opportunity, magic happens.

I've realized that giving birth to companies takes as much work, if not more, than working inside of one. My mind is constantly racing: What can I do to make it better? What new product I can offer? Where are my customers and how do I reach them? One morning as I was working to manage all of these questions by creating my to-do list, I lit a candle. It slowed me down, and I loved its beautiful lemon scent. Even more, I realized that every time I smelled that candle, I was going to remember my to-do list. Brilliant! I decided to light a candle every time I was working on my to-do list. It made a significant difference in how I went through my day.

As I took a deep breath of that lemon scent, and started to ease into my day, I looked down at my hands and thought about everything that women do with our hands on a daily basis: We give hugs, we shake hands on deals, we wipe away tears, we type e-mails, and express our love. That's when the tag line for my hand cream came to me, "Nourish your hands, nourish your world^{TM}." That morning, little did I know, I'd been given the idea for my favorite business of all, LOVE by Sarah Walton, a vegan and gluten-free skin care line, designed to remind women to take a breath and slow down.

Every day we give our best to our partners, our employers, and employees. We listen to and love our friends when they need us. We're there for our children, for our extended families and we rarely take the time to take care of ourselves. We say no to pitiful raises, fight to be the best at what we do, and we stretch ourselves to try new things. As I started to develop my hand creams, body butters, and sugar scrubs, I knew I was creating something special and new. My goal is to have a jar of my cream in every handbag in America, as a little reminder that women's needs and wants matter to me, and I'm in the game of life with all of us. As I look back on everything I've accomplished, and everything I've done and given, if I can remind women to take a breath, and remember that they matter too, that will be my favorite success. And I think of that little four-year-old girl in her grandmother's kitchen. She's learned that she matters, that her voice matters and that she deserves to enjoy moments, too.

Oh, and that raise that I asked for at the beginning of my story? I got it, and then some.

A note from Ally: *When I first met Sarah, I immediately wanted to* *be her friend. Her smile and warmth were accepting and made me feel wanted. I certainly didn't imagine that this confident, smart, and vibrant woman grew up feeling as if she didn't matter. As we grew to know each other, I was surprised to find that we share the experience of feeling alone in the world.*

Sarah is a fantastic example of a woman who sought to find her voice despite feelings of self-doubt, and an environment that didn't support her basic needs. It took some work, and a few years out in the world, but she made the conscious decision to speak up about the things that matter. This decision, and the realization that she matters (and that all women matter), is the force that drives her success. The choice to speak up is usually the first step towards making your life and your business work for you. That's exactly what Sarah did when she chose not to accept the compensation package that didn't reflect her self-worth. She used that voice to move her career from a receptionist all the way to running businesses for one of the largest tech companies in the country.

Her passion to support other women and to make all lives on this planet better is infectious. She is living proof that you can achieve anything you put your heart and mind to. That doesn't mean that it'll be easy, and you might need to take risks, but if there's one thing I take from Sarah's story, it is that this is, actually, the easier path.

Staying true to your heart and listening to your inner voice is the only way to find real, lasting, and meaningful success.

Chapter Challenge

What part of Sarah's story could you relate to the most?

_____

_____

If you could name only one thing you took away from this story, what would it be?

_____

_____

_____

What one thing will you do differently because of Sarah's story?

_____

_____

What surprised you the most in this story?

_____

_____

_____

If there was one thing you could ask Sarah, what would it be?

_____

_____

We'd love for you to connect with Sarah. If you'd like to connect with her, simply send an email to info@redefiningsuccessstories.com and put Sarah's name in the subject line.

THE REAL SPARKLY ME

Ayelet (Ally) Nathaniel

You deserve to shine, to stand out, and to be proud of who you are – even when you've been told that you are just one of many.

"Our deepest fear is not that we are inadequate. Our deepest fear is that we are powerful beyond measure." – Marianne Williamson

I was born privileged. I realize that now. I have the "right" skin color, my parents were part of the "right" political party, and I always had food, clean water, and shelter. Even so, as a child, I never felt good about myself or believed I could achieve anything in life. I didn't have a clue that people were allowed to *want* anything for themselves, let alone work hard to make it happen. I gave up on wanting things at a very young age.

I grew up in a small community in Israel called a "kibbutz." The kibbutz members, about 300 people, worked together, ate together, and raised their children together. They believed in Karl Marx's socialism, "From each according to his ability, to each according to his need," which means that people worked as much as they could and they would get what they needed: housing, food, and education. It's a specific interpretation of equality. Looking back, I think this might be a noble idea, but it didn't work very well in reality, which is why "kibbutzim" doesn't exist anymore, at least not in the same way. I was born and raised in a kibbutz and left when I was about 23 when I was told I couldn't go to the college I wanted to attend because it was too far away.

By then I was already making my own money as a quality assurance person at a small factory, and was confident I could save enough to support myself. It was one of the first decisions in my life where I trusted my instincts. It was also one of the most important decisions. By leaving, I gave up financial support and a home to come back to during the winter and summer break. I chose to leave it all behind so I could do what I wanted to do: study business management and psychology. As a result, during my college years I didn't have a "home" to go to. My parents had moved to Prague, and the kibbutz wasn't my home anymore.

Maybe you're still wondering exactly what a kibbutz is like.

Visualize a small community filled with one-story houses, big lawns, plenty of pine trees, and not many cars. In the center of the community there's a big dining hall with a kitchen. There's also an area where people can gather, chat, and enjoy a cup of coffee and a cookie, we called it "The Club." Next to The Club there's a "theater" where people can watch a movie once a week and the kids can watch TV. It was the '70s and we didn't have TV in the Children's House, where we lived. Not far from The Club are the Babies' and Children's Houses. That's where we, the children, lived. Our parents had what we called "a room." It was a very small apartment with one small bedroom and a small living room. The kitchen hardly had enough space for more than two people at a time and there were no extra rooms. Extra space wasn't needed because we didn't eat or spend much time there, that's what the public areas were for.

The kibbutz members believed that children should be raised by a (hopefully) trained adult, even if that adult wasn't the child's biological parent. They believed that if you take a child away from her parents and put her under the supervision of a trained adult, it would be better than a parent's supervision because parents aren't trained or qualified to take care of children. These people wanted to give the children the best of the best, more than they had. For example, the food the children ate was better than the food the adults ate. To maintain that system the kids were raised in Babies' Houses and later on in Children's Houses.

I was sent to the Baby House when I was three weeks old. Those first three weeks of my life were the only time in my entire life that I got to sleep next to my parents. In this system, a mother was allowed to leave her job, the same job she went back to only three weeks after her baby was born, in the middle of the day for what was called a "love hour." I watched my own mother do this with my five siblings after me. During this "love hour" a mother could nurse the baby or just spend time with her children. When the hour was over she went back to work. This flexibility was allowed because the kibbutz was so small that it wouldn't take more than ten minutes to go from one side to the other, and the Baby House was in the center of the community.

I grew up very detached, both emotionally and physically. I lacked the warmth of a loving parent's hugs. I never felt that anyone truly cared for me, or that I was important to anyone else. I lived in a group of six babies with two caregivers, and later on I was part of a group of 14 children with two caregivers who were in charge of our well-being. Years later, my parents told me that they never felt good about leaving me alone during the night. My mom would wake up early in the morning, waiting in her bed until the "official" time she could show up at the Baby House and nurse me. My dad would lie on the floor next to my crib and rock it gently until I fell asleep.

Unfortunately, I don't remember those moments. I remember feeling lonely, isolated, and invisible.

We didn't have money. We didn't need it. We got our food at the communal dining room, our clothes from the communal clothes warehouse, our shoes from the shoemaking workshop, and our schools and field trips were funded by the kibbutz and the government. The first time I held money in my hand was around the age of seven. We had guests from "the city." They had a Volkswagen Beetle, and they took us to the nearest town to eat ice cream. My parents gave me coins to pay for my ice cream. I still remember how confused and excited I felt when I held those coins. I remember the weight of them and how sad I was to let them go, even if it was for an ice cream. We had always been told that money wasn't important, but no one really told us how we paid for necessities like electricity, food, and clothes. My relationship with money started that day.

As an entrepreneur in spirit, I've had to make peace with this confusion and lack of instruction about money before I was able to ask people to pay for my services, and it wasn't easy. I had to work through the old beliefs about money and my own fears about not being important or worthy. As soon as I started working, those feelings came right up to the surface. Having my own businesses was a great opportunity to work through these old feelings. I became a pastry chef and opened a cake decorating business and I was an editor and writer for a pregnancy and childbirth online magazine where I got to support thousands of women. And before becoming an entrepreneur I worked for one of the biggest high-tech companies in Israel as a recruiter. I remember jumping up and whooping with joy when I got their compensation offer. It was so much more than I believed I was worth. Over time, I've learned to recognize these older beliefs, and let them go.

When my husband and I moved to the United States with our two children, my career came to a standstill. I had to figure out what to do next. My first job here was at a chocolate shop, which I left when my third child was born and I had to reinvent myself again. I started a new business called "Playful Kitchen" where I taught children baking and cooking classes. I'm proud to say that my programs are still running during the summer months. Starting this little business gave me the confidence and courage to keep going, and I owe my success today to those early days of creating menus, curriculums, and learning how to share my expertise. The first check I got was for $50 and I remember feeling so proud and accomplished. Since then I've learned how to ask for what I'm worth and I'm about to publish a cookbook for children.

Back in the kibbutz, we were taught that hard work was of the highest value, and we were expected to work from a very young age. In our Children's House we made the beds, cleaned the dishes, polished shoes, washed the floors, and folded laundry. As we aged, the tasks changed as we headed into the local factory or into agriculture. We picked fruit: oranges, kiwi, and pears. We would weed the cotton and tomato fields. We were expected to wake up very early, around 5:00 a.m., before the brutal Israeli sun would burn our skin, and work until 2:00 p.m. This is one habit I've taken with me; I still like to wake up early. During high school, we had a working day once a week as part of our curriculum. I worked in many different places: I was a landscaper, a baby-sitter, I worked in a plastic factory, a hot dog factory, our communal kitchen, and I raised fish, hamsters, and birds, and worked in the fields.

We were also taught to value creativity. Since we didn't have money we offered handmade birthday gifts to each other. We learned how to knit, sew, embroider, and weave. We had four hours of art and crafts lessons, twice a week from 2:00 p.m. to 4:00 p.m. Those hours are where I learned woodwork, macramé, basket weaving, and much more. We were expected to use our hands to create products, and to work the land. I believe that my ability to solve problems easily is a direct result of those art and crafts lessons. Solving problems while using your hands wires the brain to have that ability.

When I was five years old I had a single moment in school that shaped my self-perception for years to come. In a rare moment of closeness with my dad, he taught me how to read. We spent time together sitting on the bed in my parents' room, learning the Hebrew letters and putting letters into sentences. I was so proud of my ability to learn quickly! I felt powerful and capable. When I went back to the classroom, at the Children's House, all I wanted to do was to show the teacher and the other kids how much I knew. I was excited, proud of myself, and enthusiastic to share my newfound wisdom with the world.

During our lessons that day, I raised my hand several times when the teacher asked the class to recognize letters. But I didn't get permission to answer. Maybe the teacher didn't call on me because I was the youngest in the classroom, or maybe it was because I was a girl. I remember feeling that boys got more attention and were expected to know more than the girls, even though we were told we were all are equal. I have no way to know why she didn't call on me that day, but feeling very frustrated I couldn't take it anymore. The next time she asked us to raise our hands if we knew a letter, I couldn't stop myself and I shouted, "Lamed!" (the Hebrew letter L). She looked at me and said, "If you know so much, there's no reason for you to stay here. Please leave the classroom." Shocked and confused, I got up and walked out of the room. I sat outside feeling isolated and separate because I had shared my knowledge. Another teacher saw my tears and let me back into the classroom. I was told that my teacher didn't know how much it would hurt me to leave, so

I went back in. But I'd learned my lesson: Never show how much you know, or you will be humiliated and isolated. I was confronted with this fear as I was publishing my number one best seller, *Sparkly Me*. It's hard for me to describe how much courage it took to release that book. I had to recognize that I'm not that little girl anymore and that it's OK to share myself with the rest of the world.

When I was six years old, my parents decided to move to another kibbutz. I know they told me about it in advance, but the feeling at the time was that I didn't get any notice. One day there were boxes, and the next day I was asked to climb into a truck that took us to our new home. I was taken away from my friends and from everything I knew. I was expected to make friends with new children, to adapt to new teachers and a new bed as if it was no big deal. I felt estranged among the new kids, whom I didn't know at all. I didn't know the rules. I didn't know their games or the group dynamics. My parents weren't around and I didn't have anyone to call or ask for help when I didn't feel like asking strangers. The feelings of isolation and loneliness got stronger every day. I gained weight and became the chubby tomboy. I felt that there was nothing good about me and I blamed myself for not being good enough to be popular. I was bullied for the way I looked for years, until seventh grade. Thankfully being a good student gave me some kind of confidence.

The kibbutz separated us from our parents for most of the day. We got to be with our parents from 4:00 p.m. to 7:00 p.m. every day, but that was it. This separation was intended to make us feel that we were all the same. No one was preferred over another. But it also made me feel like there was nothing special about me. I was never told that I was smart, beautiful, or loved. We weren't supposed to feel unique in any way. I'm aware that these feelings might not be the same for all the kids that were in my kibbutz and I'm sure some parents made their children feel special. Unfortunately, I never felt that way.

I do have one memory of feeling special, before we left our first kibbutz. I had an "older sister," Efrat. She wasn't my biological sister, but she was part of my family for a short time. She was in her 20s, about the same age as my parents, and she spent a lot of time with my family. For my sixth birthday she wrote a short children's book about me. I was the main character. I was the center of attention! What a new feeling! She illustrated the book by herself, thinking just about me as she created it. I could tell she loved me and that I was special to her. Efrat was an American who lived in Israel for only a short time. Thinking of her even today helps me remember that I'm unique, special, and lovable. Maybe she's the reason why I love both this country and children's books.

When we were in seventh grade I moved to a new school. It was a boarding school located in another kibbutz, 20 minutes away from where my parents lived. Now I got to be with my parents twice a week for a couple of hours each time, and that was the only time I could see them. I had a room at the boarding school where I lived with two other girls. I was surrounded by other kids all day long and I can't remember a quiet or private time. We had active social lives with very little adult supervision. We studied, ate, and spent our spare time together. But despite all of that time with other kids, I still felt lonely. I felt like there was no one out there to care for me, I didn't know how anyone could see me among the crowd.

A few years ago, when I was looking for a publisher for the children's cookbook I'm about to launch, these same feelings came into play again. I knew they were going to stop me from being successful, especially if I let myself believe that I'm not special, worthy, and capable. I figured out that feeling like this wasn't going to serve me at all, and that these feelings aren't based on my current reality. At the time I had a working business and I'd raised three young children at the same time. What would I call that if not success? As I worked through my old feelings, I came to understand that it was up to me to train my brain to see *today's* reality. Not the reality I experienced as a young girl. So I wrote ten affirmations and repeated them to myself every morning when I woke up and every night before I went to sleep.

I had to rewire my brain to my new reality; I'm great just as I am, and I have the power and ability to be as successful as I want to be:

"I'm choosing to believe the people who tell me how smart, talented and lovable I am."

And I practiced this daily. Every time I got a compliment I *chose* to believe it.

The rest of the work came when I had to let go of the feeling that I'm alone in this world. I believe this was absolutely crucial for me to move forward and become successful. I had to trust that there is help out there, even though as a young child I didn't have it. To strengthen this new muscle, I chose two good friends that I could rely upon, and I practiced asking for help. I'm happy to tell you, it worked.

In fact, this affirmation and practice worked so well for me, that I decided to test it out on other things I wanted in my life, and I created a new goal: to publish a cookbook and become a best-selling author.

Here's the affirmation I wrote for this one:

"I love being a best-selling author."

I didn't realize when I created this affirmation that I actually wasn't going to publish the cookbook. Instead, I published a lovely children's book, *Sparkly Me*, which became my best-selling book.

In fact, it was on Amazon's Best Seller list for over 16 weeks. So while the path may have been different than I thought it was when I created the affirmation, the affirmation worked. I certainly can't complain.

Growing up the way I did has left me with a deep compassion for those around me who may be feeling lonely or incapable. I know how awful that is. Writing a book can feel like a daunting task, and I know that has kept many capable and talented people from even getting started, which is why I started my business. I know how important it is for a budding author to step out of her shell and show the world who she really is. I've been there, both as a child and as a best-selling author, and I know how lonely it can be. I want to make sure no one else ever feels that way as they move towards sharing their stories with the world.

"We ask ourselves, who am I to be brilliant, gorgeous, talented, and fabulous? Actually, who are you not to be?" – Marianne Williamson

Note from Sarah: Ally's story pulled at emotions in me that I didn't expect to feel while reading a book about success. We decided to put our stories next to each other in this book because we found we had a common theme: feeling alone. I can imagine what it was like to grow up feeling like one of many, almost invisible, but I've watched

Ally turn that feeling into her strength as she lovingly pours herself into children's books and her own children. My daughter loves Ally's bestseller Sparkly Me and reads it almost daily. The book elicits the opposite of every feeling Ally felt growing up; it allows for feeling special, for wanting what's beautiful, and for standing out in the crowd.

When I think of Ally's example of success, I think of a woman creating her own path, through trial and error by finding her own voice, mothering and nurturing herself, and rising to every occasion she's been handed. In her soft, gentle way, she's conquered some of the hardest obstacles that women can face, and she's done it with grace.

Like all of the women in this book, Ally has bucked the circumstances she was given, created her own way, and is now looking to bring as many women as she can with her. She's an incredible example of the quiet, fierce strength of women.

Chapter Challenge

What part of Ally's story could you relate to the most?

_____

_____

If you could name only one thing you took away from this story, what would it be?

_____

_____

_____

What one thing will you do differently because of Ally's story?

_____

_____

What surprised you the most in this story?

_____

_____

_____

If there was one thing you could ask Ally, what would it be?

_____

_____

We'd love for you to connect with Ally. If you'd like to connect with her, simply send an email to info@redefiningsuccessstories.com and put Ally's name in the subject line.

LIVE

Renee Jensen

We all have struggles that we don't think anyone else will understand. But we're all in this life together, and sometimes our biggest triumph is greeting a new day with hope.

"The vibrations of mental forces are the finest and consequently the most powerful in existence." – *Charles Haanel*

Success to me is falling down and getting back up. It's about falling down multiple times and choosing to rise from each fall. It's about embracing that we are all imperfectly perfect. It's screaming at the top of your lungs, "I will *not* go down without a fight and I will never ever stay down no matter what!"

Five years ago my ex-husband, Tom, and I fell on very hard times.

During these times, we both fell in love with other people. Tom married the woman he fell in love with, they have a beautiful baby girl, have another baby on the way, and my children have a wonderful stepmom. The man I fell in love with, Andy, the man who was my best friend and my rock through the end of my marriage, took his own life. The morning of his death, he came to my house to say his last goodbyes. "Thank you for everything you did for me," he said. I listened to his old Subaru pull away and eight hours later he was gone.

I was about to close my business and was facing financial ruin. The overwhelming experience of failure, depression, lack of sleep, caring for an infant and a three-year-old sent me in to a downward spiral, from which I almost didn't recover. Four months later, the lack of sleep and depression caused my brain to shut down. I couldn't remember my own phone number. I couldn't read Dr. Seuss's *Cat in the Hat* to my kids. It was like having Alzheimer's at the age of 33.

I contemplated suicide three separate times. I didn't just think about it, I had a plan: death by Jeep and gas, by Jeep and mountain cliff, by Xanax. The first time was less than a week after Andy died. I was ready to put myself in the garage with my Jeep running. I had the sense to call Tom and ask him to take the kids for a couple of weeks so I could get my head back on straight. He came and got them and they spent several weeks with their dad in New Jersey. I missed my son's first birthday, but the best gift I could have given to him was my life.

Divine intervention has always come to my aid through my best friend Kara and my two amazing children, Grace and Dominic. I would see those precious babies in my mind and I'd say, "Fuck this" and I'd get it together. I made the decision to "not make that decision" three times in six months. Several months after Andy's death, I spent a week in a psychiatric hospital, after which I chose to leave my children with Tom for six weeks, so I could head to Jackson Hole and get my physical and mental health back on track. It's the hardest decision I've ever made.

Within 12 hours of making this "do or die" decision, I left my children not knowing what the consequences of "abandoning" them might be. I climbed into a cab at 4:30 in the morning and cried for the next eight hours until I reached the place that would help me heal. After those six weeks, I decided to move to New Jersey with less than $2,000 to my name, no job, and my trusty Jeep. It was time to reclaim my place in this world as a mother and a woman with a purpose. I was determined to make my life a success.

My story starts long before Tom and I fell in love with other people. I was born in South Korea, where there is no record of my birth. I

105

was found as an infant and placed in an orphanage. Lee Sang Sook was the name that was chosen for me, and November 11, 1976, was the birthday I was given. In July of 1977, I was adopted by my American parents and raised in a small town in northeast Illinois as one of five children: three of us are adopted and two are my parents' biological children.

My mother was told she would never be able to have children "of her own." Had she known she could have her own children when she saw my picture in the Holt International brochure, she would have thought, "Oh, poor baby. I hope some nice family will give her a home." Then she would've tossed the magazine out and never given me another thought. Instead, at seven months old, I was flown in a 747 across the Pacific and halfway around the world.

I wish I had a different story to tell you about my adoptive parents. It sounds so nice initially, doesn't it? In theory I should have been the answered prayer of a barren couple. Instead I grew up knowing I was a burden. My father worked hard day in and day out while my mom took care of all of us. She had no friends nearby. I know now how hard that must have been for her. Mental illness ran in my mother's family, and I'm sure that contributed to her behavior, but it was no secret that my mother didn't care for me. Her specific words were, "You're worthless and you'll end up dead in a gutter someday."

I left home a couple of months after I graduated from high school with no money and garbage bags filled with my clothes. My childhood friend, Heather, and her family took me in for several months. After I found myself a decent job, I got my own apartment and I spent over a decade in survival mode. I worked very hard to prove my mother wrong. I was going to succeed. Dying in the gutter was *not* my fate. In my mind, if I didn't succeed she would win. I held a handful of pretty decent jobs but all the while, I completely ignored my past. I was in and out of relationships, some good but most pretty unhealthy. I was searching for love in the wrong places. The concept of unconditional love was foreign to me until I became a mother.

When I landed in New Jersey in my trusty Jeep, I knew it was time to start over. I had chosen not to ask Tom for alimony during our divorce. He took care of the childcare, health insurance, and the kids' school and medical expenses, for which I'm grateful. But I wanted to do the rest on my own. I worked as hard as I could to provide for my children and me. We started out in a single bedroom (literally one room), then we shared a house with another divorced woman for three and a half years. The kids and I shared a large bedroom. Grace had her own bed and Dominic and I would sleep in the larger bed until I had enough money for bunk beds. It wasn't perfect but we made it work.

After living with other people for over four years, I was able to afford my own apartment. Every year has become better and easier. I had six different jobs in those four years, and every new job came with a better salary, better benefits, and a more flexible schedule. I fought through it all and found my purpose in life: to share my experiences and create awareness around the importance of mental health and wellness for mothers.

To that end, I created the "Bergen County Mommies TIME OUT" (BCMTO) Facebook page. It's one of my greatest accomplishments to date. As I re-examined my life and my goals, something was missing: friendship with other women and other mothers. Without any intention of starting the BCMTO page, I posted on another Facebook page, "Hey, if anyone wants to get a drink or an appetizer, let me know." I knew I needed friends, so I reached out to find some.

Fifty women, all strangers for the most part, attended that first event. As I was looking around the room, I noticed that not one woman was on her cell phone. Everyone was fully engaged in conversation. I felt a wave of emotion come over me thinking about the bonds that were being formed there right in front of me, all from a post on a Facebook page. I knew that these newly forming relationships might save someone else one day when faced with hardship, grief, or tragedy. I also knew that those friendships would bring joy and happiness, a kind of security and sense of fulfillment that we don't get from significant others or our children. It's a different kind of unconditional love, and all women need it. Today we schedule weekly meet-ups or what I lovingly call a "Time Out" event, so moms can step outside the box of the day-to-day to meet other women. I know from experience that it "takes a village." My girlfriends saved my life and I know this group of women can ultimately do the same for each other.

"Here's to the crazy ones, the misfits, the troublemakers, the round pegs in the square holes. While some of you may see them as crazy, we see them as genius." – Steve Jobs

On December 6, 2010, I signed myself in to Bergen Regional Medical Center in Paramus in New Jersey. My ex-sister-in-law, Jen, drove me to the hospital on that cold dreary morning. An hour earlier, she and Tom had asked me if I wanted to get admitted so I could get "checked out." I was totally on board. I was under the impression that I was going to see legitimate specialists who could fix whatever was wrong with my brain.

On the way to the hospital, I sat in the passenger seat of Jen's BMW being chauffeured to what I hoped would be some answers. As we were driving, Jen asked me if I was suicidal. I didn't answer, I just cried quietly. As we passed through the entrance of Bergen Regional there was absolutely no indication that I was about to commit myself to a mental health facility. It didn't look like a scary facility with doctors and nurses in white coats caring for crazy people. It didn't have "Loony Bin" marked on the entrance sign at the gates. It looked like a nice, normal hospital.

It had been many years or abandonment issues that landed me in the passenger seat of that BMW. After the separation, the financial ruin and Andy's suicide, my body was shutting down. I felt like the world was closing in on me. I had suffered a stress-induced isolated seizure and for the next two months my brain had refused to work properly. I tried to keep it together for the kids, but I was raising a three-year-old and one-year-old by myself. Tom had stopped sending us money, so I had cashed out my retirement account, but I had no idea how we were going to survive once that money was gone. I beat myself up over our separation. I replayed every minute of every day leading up to Andy's suicide.

I was on the phone in Jackson Hole when the seizure hit. As I was talking with my friend, she heard the phone drop to the ground. She figured one of the kids had grabbed the phone, and she didn't call back. Forty-five minutes later I woke up discombobulated. Tom was in town visiting, and was out with Grace, but I didn't understand why his backpack and Yankee hat were sitting on the floor in the corner of my bedroom. I couldn't figure out how to operate my phone. I started to panic and was pacing the floor. I heard Dominic wake up from his nap and I snapped out of it. I ran upstairs and picked him up and we rushed over to my friend's house. I walked in and handed her my phone and couldn't stop crying. After a few minutes, she looked at her husband and said, "Something is really wrong." She called Tom and told him to come back with Grace. He was irritated with me and believed that I was only trying to get attention.

I went to lie down and realized that my mouth hurt. I looked in the bathroom mirror at my tongue and saw that it was lacerated. That's when I realized I'd had a seizure. Tom took me to the ER where they administered a few tests but couldn't find anything. He stayed in town for a week and took me to a neurologist for more tests, but they couldn't find anything either. Tom left at the end of the week and my health continued to deteriorate. I had lost all depth perception and my senses were numb.

Four weeks later I was lying in a hospital bed: diagnosed, re-diagnosed, misdiagnosed, Epstein-Barr, West Nile, viral meningitis. I had two spinal taps in 24 hours when the Teton Valley physicians decided I had bacterial meningitis and put me in isolation for three days. When they let me out, I was told I never had meningitis. During all of this, Tom, his family, and the hospital staff were making plans to have me commit myself to Bergen Regional.

When we left the hospital, Tom, the kids, and I spent a couple of nights with my best friend Kara and her family. Kara had to spoon-feed me because I was so out of it. I could hear Tom on the phone in the next room talking to his family. I didn't hear the exact words, but I remember thinking that he was going to have me locked up and throw away the key. That night when everyone was asleep, I put my jacket and boots on and paced the front foyer plotting my suicide. There was no way in hell I was going to let him have me locked up. We were separated, not divorced, and he still had the legal right to have me committed. But the next day when Tom asked me if I wanted to fly back east to get checked out by "real" doctors, I thought, "Hallelujah. He's finally on board."

When Jen's BMW pulled up to Bergen Regional, we went in through the emergency room because I didn't have health insurance at the time. As I was doing the paperwork, a woman asked for my Social Security number and I started to cry. I fumbled to find my license and my Social Security card because I couldn't remember what it was.

We waited for hours for a room to open up. During the wait, police officers were coming in with people on stretchers. One of the nurses gave me an Ativan to calm me down because I was starting to get agitated by all the "activity." I was getting nervous and I turned to Jen, "Is this a regular hospital?" She said, "Yeah, they have a neurological department. They have a pediatrics and a maternity wing, too." I believed her. When a doctor finally arrived, he asked Jen to give us some privacy. My brain wasn't processing correctly, but I think he was asking me if I knew what I was signing. Silent tears rolled down my face as I signed the form. I trusted Jen. I trusted Tom. And I trusted their family. The last thing I saw was Jen's face as they wheeled me away.

During the first couple of days, I was a little out of it but I made a couple of observations. The doors to get off the floor were locked. When I was "allowed" to go outside, the courtyard had very high fences. At night as I stared out my window across the courtyard into other people's rooms, I looked for children or babies. "Oh shit. I know where I am." The light bulb finally went on. I had voluntarily involuntarily checked myself in to a mental health facility. I spent the next several days in and out of group sessions. The doctors and nurses rarely checked on me. All of the patients asked me why I was there. Apparently there are a lot of people who were sicker than I was, and I appeared to be "normal." I did everything I could to get released including begging God for help. I didn't realize I'd signed a 72-hour observation form. I could have left after three days. I stayed for seven.

It was after that visit that I took the six weeks in Jackson Hole to heal. Tom and his family were pushing me to make decisions about where I was going to live, work, and what I was going to do next. I felt consumed by the pressure. I knew Tom's mother kept Xanax in her purse, so I crept over to her bag and took it out. I gave her a hug and went up to the bathroom. I thought of my children, looked at myself in the mirror and said, "Renee, take a shower. You'll feel better." I put the pills back in her purse and took a shower. I called Kara, who said, "You need to get out of there. Now. You're either going to end up dead or back in that hospital." I told her I couldn't leave the kids. She reassured me that the kids would be fine and that I needed to get healthy again.

It only took one week back in Jackson Hole for me to start to feel healthy. No doctors. No medication. No massive amounts of sleep. Everyone has his or her own beliefs, but for me, it felt like divine intervention brought me back; divine intervention through my closest girlfriends, to whom I've dedicated the Mommies TIME OUT page. Six weeks later, I was on my way back to New Jersey to start over.

I'm not the definition of success by "normal" standards. My net worth is near zero. I'm divorced with two children. I live in a one-bedroom apartment above a pub that is currently under construction. But I'm alive, and I'm *happy*. The initial reaction when I share this story is, "Oh OK," followed by an uncomfortable silence. But I don't let that reaction stop me from talking. I believe in faith, hope, and love. I've learned that successfully emerging from hardship and pain is a state of mind, and we're all stronger when we share the truth. And there is no magic bullet, it takes daily practice, care and attention to pull positive thoughts into my life and let the bad go. But I do it, and it works.

I would have never pulled out of that darkness if it weren't for the loves in my life: my children, my girlfriends, and God. My girlfriends supported me through it all; they didn't judge, they loved. And I've found the same kind of friendships through the BCMTO page. Every time I think of Andy, I know that even though it was his time to go, it wasn't mine. I have a whole lot of life to live, love to give, and light to emit to those who are lost. Being a woman and a mother is no easy task. But we were born into this world for a reason. And I know that if I can come back from the brink of a nervous breakdown, suicidal thoughts, and deep depression, any of us can face what life gives us.

Success is not about the fancy car you drive or how many zeroes are at the end of your paycheck. Success is defined by how hard you worked to acquire that fancy car or those extra zeroes at the end of your paycheck. It's about being grateful and positively touching as many lives as you can. Don't ever give up and greet every day with gratitude. Find your purpose, even if you have to dig deep, because you have one. We all do.

A note from Sarah and Ally: When Sarah first met Renee at a networking event, her bright smile and contagious happiness were what stood out. It's immediately apparent that she cares about the person she's talking to, she's truly interested in other people, and she's here to make a difference for as many women as she can. Her smile will make you smile, and she is full of energy, vibrant with life, and incredibly warm.

Upon first meeting Renee, you would never know that she's struggled with dark moments, and that one of her biggest triumphs to date is that she's still alive. We knew that Renee's story would become one of the more important in our book as it falls into the hands of women everywhere who are facing the unbearable. We have no control over what life will hand us, but we always have control over how we respond to it. This story illustrates that better than most. And we want to personally thank Renee for her courage, grit, and generosity in sharing her darkest moments, and her true definition of success, which bucks everything we've been taught as women. We see this definition of success as simple: LIVE.

Every life matters, everyone is here to share their unique talents, insights, and experiences with others. We need each other, and sometimes it's up to us to create the communities we need to flourish. Just because things aren't handed to us on a silver platter, doesn't mean we don't deserve them. The point is to get up, get out there, and share ourselves with a world that is hungry for our specific gifts.

Chapter Challenge

What part of Renee's story could you relate to the most?

_____

_____

If you could name only one thing you took away from this story, what would it be?

_____

_____

_____

What one thing will you do differently because of Renee's story?

_____

_____

What surprised you the most in this story?

_____

_____

_____

If there was one thing you could ask Renee, what would it be?

_____

_____

We'd love for you to connect with Renee. If you'd like to connect with her, simply send an email to info@redefiningsuccessstories.com and put Renee's name in the subject line.

NO ONE CAN STOP YOU BUT YOU

Beth Donalds

Sometimes, the love of one woman is all it takes.

Let me start by saying that I believe in grand plans. That's not to say we don't have choices, we absolutely have choices. But I believe that those choices just take us closer or further away from where we're supposed to be, and in the end, we always end up in the right place. So I'll just let that sink in while I tell you my story.

Three years ago I left my corporate job. I knew it was time for me to share the knowledge I acquired throughout my career and help small businesses and female entrepreneurs create the strategic and operational processes necessary to develop and grow a business. I can't really say it was a full-blown plan. I just knew I wanted to help

119

people realize that they are business owners first. And here's what I mean by that: Let's say you're at a networking event and you meet someone who says, "Hi, I'm Nancy, I'm a realtor." What I want her to say is, "Hi, I'm Nancy. I'm a business owner, and my product is real estate."

The distinction is subtle, but it displays a completely different mindset. If you say, "I'm a realtor," that's it. That's all you do. You sell houses. But if you say, "I'm a business owner," what you're really saying is that at some point in the future you'll have a staff, and maybe more realtors working for you. You're creating a business, a company. There's a big difference between owning a business and doing tasks. Selling houses is a task. When you own the business, you ask questions like: "Where is my customer, how do I court that customer, how do I market, how do I grow my business, how do I expand, how do I pay the rent?" Business owners think about their businesses all the time. People who are doing tasks don't think that way.

Women who go into business often think of business as a task, and not as creating a company. I consider it my job to guide women towards the understanding that there is a natural transition from performing tasks to running a business. It's okay to start out doing everything on your own, to do the tasks you love doing. But as the business grows, you'll begin to discover that you can't do it all.

You're going to run out of time, money, or energy if you don't hire someone else to help. You may need someone to help with the administrative tasks. Then maybe you'll need to partner with someone, or hire more staff.

The bigger the business gets, the less time there is to do the things you did when you started the business. In growing, you will become more of the owner and less of a task doer. For some people that's good; for others, they're getting away from what they love and it doesn't make them happy. I think a lot of people, especially women, don't really think this through.

Part of that has to do with the roles we play in society. When it comes to business, men and women are very different. There are hundreds of books written about this and they probably say it better than I do. The reality is that while much has changed over the past few decades, men are still considered the breadwinners and women's income is secondary. When kids come along, the woman will give up her job because it isn't as important or as valued. Women who decide to go into business, because they're at home or they have a passion or their kids are grown, aren't necessarily thinking, "This is going to be a career and I'm going to build an empire." They're thinking, "Oh, extra pocket money," or "I'll keep myself busy."

I help women shift this mindset by working through all of these details and mapping them out. When I ask most women what their three-year plan is, they don't have an answer. But if I ask the same question to a man, whose family is relying on his income, he'll have an answer. I help change that, and my work with women is focused on processes that help them come up with these answers, too.

When I decided to leave corporate America, where you can make a lot of money but not necessarily make a difference, I wasn't entirely sure how I was going to make a living. For a woman whose one clear goal in life was to earn money and be self-sufficient, this was quite a departure. But the truth is I'd reached a point where that goal was no longer working for me. I wanted to say to the cosmos, "I have been blessed. Thank you." and pay it forward.

I knew that I was going to be helping 20 families at a time. I knew that the children of these families would be able to go to college because of the work we were going to do together. Over the years I've seen so many women trying to go into business with no support, and they were failing miserably. I wanted to improve their odds of success. I knew I could do it. So I did.

But I'm not going to lie – this has been the largest leap of faith I've ever taken. I left an extremely lucrative job to do this without knowing how it would happen. Now when I ask my clients to take a leap of faith, I completely get how hard that is. You can have all the numbers, all the plans in place, and I can show you how it will all work and tell you you'll be OK. But ultimately, that first step takes a serious amount of courage.

Which leads me to my childhood and my grandmother, I'll tell you more about her in the coming paragraphs. But she believed that if you really put your faith in the universe, the cosmos, or whatever you want to call it, your life will be filled with amazing opportunities – and all you have to do is say "yes." I have lived by this guiding principle and been incredibly blessed. I've seen time and again that if we are truly open to it, the grand plan will come into play throughout our lives. And we'll see how all of our decisions have come together to lead us to the place we're absolutely meant to be.

I get this faith and strength through experience, but also through my childhood. Growing up, I was very close to my grandmother. She was born in 1900 and lived to be 105. I have wonderful memories of cooking and making matzo balls from scratch with her. We would make meatballs by freshly grinding the meat at the grinder and she always made it so much fun. She had the most beautiful sense of style! And she always wore lovely jewelry. One piece I always admired had three strands, white gold, yellow gold, and pink gold. She braided the three strands into an extraordinary necklace that she would wear often and I feel so lucky that she gave it to me. I wear it whenever I have professional pictures taken.

My grandmother was a woman's libber before it was popular. She never changed her name, she never wore a wedding band, and she didn't understand why she had to. Obviously this was just unheard of at the beginning of the last century, but that's who she was. She was always paving her own way and she refused to let anyone tell her what she couldn't do. She set such an incredible example of what it means to be a woman. She used to tell me her story of being engaged to an extremely wealthy man. One day as they were riding the subway together, he walked through the turnstile in front of her without a backwards glance. She knew at that moment that this was not the man for her. But her sister was getting married in a few weeks and she didn't want to distract from her sister's big day. So she stayed engaged through the wedding, and broke off the engagement the next day.

Before this engagement, my soon-to-be grandfather would ask her out on dates often. She told him that she would never go out with him. But once she broke off the engagement, he called her one more time. Out of exasperation she said, "If I go out with you, will you stop asking?" He promised. On their first date, it was absolutely pouring rain. As they were driving to dinner, the spare tire fell off the back of his car. He pulled over and got out of the car to reattach the tire, all the while getting soaked. When he got back into the car, dripping with rain, he turned to my grandmother and asked, "Are you OK?" That's when she knew she was going to marry him. And she did. Unfortunately, he died young and they were only married for 25 years.

Their marriage was such an amazing partnership that she never married again. She had plenty of opportunities, but she knew she would never be able to replicate what they had. My grandmother had a way of trusting her instincts. She observed the world around her with confidence, and made decisions that worked for her. She always taught me that the only person who could stop me was me. She believed that anything was possible, that there wasn't anything she couldn't do because she was a woman. And she proved it every day of her life.

My grandmother reinvented her career several times throughout her life. Business minded from the time she was a girl, she worked in her parents' coffee grinding shop (think Starbucks circa the1920s) through her teens and 20s. She put in long hours, and the more she worked the more she loved it. When her father realized that she had made work such a priority, he sold the business, telling her that he if he didn't she would never get married. She continued to work part-time as an accountant after she married my grandfather, and when he died, she went back to work full-time, which wasn't exactly the norm in the 1950s. I remember visiting her in the Catskills, where she spent entire summers doing bookkeeping and accounting for the big hotels in their heyday. In the 1960s she became general manager of Le Jardin Disco in Manhattan, and for ten years, she ran the precursor to what would become Studio 54.

The most dramatic example of her irrepressible spirit was when she joined Actors' Equity at the young age of 89, and actively performed in roles for the next ten years. She figured that 99 was a good age to retire. If someone had told her that at the age of 89 she couldn't act, her response would have been, "Why not?" She was fearless and limitless, and she never really had a grand plan. But when a good opportunity presented itself, she'd always say yes.

As a young girl, I followed in her footsteps. I went about my life making choices, but I did so without a larger picture in mind. I believe we all do that, actually, whether we're aware of it or not. A lot of what we believe is coincidence is actually that larger picture coming together. I knew from a very early age that I wanted my own income and to be self-sufficient. I wanted that more than I wanted any particular career. So I went out and got my first job when I was in the third grade. My lifelong friend Anita and I shared a paper route. We would pick up our papers after school, get on our bicycles, and hand-deliver those papers for two hours. Since then, there has never been a time when I didn't have my own source of income. I knew that I had the talent and knowledge to maintain my independence. I started delivering newspapers because it didn't

126

require a specific skill. I just needed to ride a bike and I knew I could do that. So I did.

It wasn't lack that drove me. My grandmother always indulged me in anything and everything I wanted, whether it was music lessons, clothes, or jewelry. I just knew that I wanted to be self-reliant. I got my working papers when I was 16 and went to every store in our town in search of a job. I got two offers: One was at a dry cleaners and the other the local pharmacy. I took the job at the pharmacy because the dry cleaners required that I clean the toilets. Sometimes we just have to be practical.

I worked at the pharmacy three or four days a week all through high school. I was in charge of medical records, handwriting and updating the patients' files. I worked my junior and senior year, and then the pharmacy hired me for the summers, too. That was when I realized I loved saving money. Some people get joy from spending money; I get joy from watching it grow and accumulate. This future nest egg would allow me to pursue my future passions.

During this time in high school, I had fallen in love with singing. I wanted to take it seriously, so I continued to go to school full-time, and three times a week I would get on a bus and go to the Manhattan School of Music. At the age of 16, I was on buses at the Port Authority at 11:00 p.m., heading home from voice lessons. Looking back, I realize that this probably wasn't the safest thing I ever did, but no one was going to tell me I couldn't do it. I made that trek until I went to college, where I majored in voice.

The summer between my freshman and sophomore year of college, I headed to Europe to tour on the road. We traveled through Russia and Romania. And while it was an amazing experience, I realized that I didn't want to live on a bus for the rest of my life. I knew I had a good voice, but not a great voice. Great voices sing at the Met and at La Scala. Good voices spend their lives on buses. I ended my road trip knowing I had to change my major. I decided that if I wasn't going to pursue my passion then I was going to make money. So I decided to go into accounting. It wasn't part of a plan, but my mother, my stepfather, and my grandmother were all accountants. It was something I grew up with and I knew I'd be good at it. If I couldn't do what I loved, I was going to do what I was good at.

After graduation, I worked locally in small businesses for a few years. I knew I had to get my CPA, but I didn't know if I could pass that horrible test. Instead I got an MBA at Fairleigh Dickinson University, where some wonderfully honest people told me I still needed to get my CPA. So I locked myself in a room for three months and I studied. I studied harder than I've ever studied for anything. I was nervous, but finally the day came. I sat for the test, and I passed! It was the hardest thing I've ever done, and I'll never do it again. I will renew that license until the day I die.

Newly armed with an MBA and a CPA, I headed into Manhattan and embarked on a wonderful new career. Sometimes I sought change, and sometimes change sought me. Many times a recruiter would call and say, "Hey, I have a new opening, are you interested?" And I would jump at the new opportunity. I had my credentials and I was satisfied with that. I never had the desire to be the vice president, to be at the top, or to hit certain milestones by certain times in my life. I worked hard and I did great work. So when opportunity found me, who was I to say no?

For the bulk of my career I worked for Japanese companies. Unbeknownst to me, the Japanese had issues with working women in positions of authority. Most Japanese women go to work to find their future husbands and then they leave the business world once they get married. It was such a contrast to the example my grandmother had set for me. When I started working for these companies, I would see men in suits, and women in schoolgirl uniforms. Women were not taken seriously, and it was very clear they were subservient. I learned about these cultural differences by talking to the women about how they felt, and what their goals were. The men would glare at me in the beginning, but I didn't let that stop me. As time passed, those men ended up trusting me, and coming to me for advice about American culture and how to ingratiate themselves into American business. Although I didn't fully realize it at the time, this was a turning point in my career, and in my life.

Throughout this time, I stayed true to myself, and my values. I worked hard, and I always did the best job I could, but I never lost sight of what my grandmother had taught me by her example. I never noticed a glass ceiling, nor did I act like one existed. As time passed, I ended up being the only female board member in my company. By many people's standards this meant I had "arrived," "made it to the top," "was a huge success." But I wasn't happy. The joy had gone out of my life. I was 55 years old, and I knew something had to change. Grand plan or no grand plan, there are moments when you need to step back and say to yourself, "Is this it? Is this what I want to do for the rest of my life?" There were a few times, when I was in my early 50s, where I'd think, "I don't want to do this anymore." But at 55, it was the first time I consciously took hold of my career and said, "I am *not* going to do this anymore."

And that's how I started my business, teaching women to shift their mindsets about their companies. I feel so lucky that my unplanned plan has led me to this place. I've learned so much through my experiences with work, studying to earn my CPA, teaching men of different cultures how to treat women, watching my grandmother always go after what she wanted, and ultimately, being reminded of her words, "No one can stop you but you."

A note from Sarah and Ally: *After reading Beth's story, we all want a grandmother like hers! What a woman! But what makes Beth's story so great is that she listened to what her grandmother taught her, she took it on as her own, and she has kept it with her all her life. That's the difference between success and mediocrity: accepting the lessons others teach us, and applying them to ourselves.*

We love the example that Beth gives for women and how we think about business. There are subtle shifts in what she shares, but they're vitally important. Learning to alter our thinking about our day-to-day tasks makes a world of difference in what we end up creating.

But above all, there's one thing about Beth's story that we hope you take away: Sometimes, it only takes one woman to make the difference for another. What if Beth had a different grandmother? What if her grandmother didn't take the time to share her stories? That's where the magic truly lies, in being the one woman who truly makes a difference. While all of us should strive to find the lessons in life generously shared by those around us, we should also seek to be the person who shares and be the woman who lifts up those around her. If it only takes one woman to make a difference, then we should all strive to be that woman for those we love.

Chapter Challenge

What part of Beth's story could you relate to the most?

_____

_____

If you could name only one thing you took away from this story, what would it be?

_____

_____

_____

What one thing will you do differently because of Beth's story?

_____

_____

What surprised you the most in this story?

_____

_____

If there was one thing you could ask Beth, what would it be?

_____

_____

We'd love for you to connect with Beth. If you'd like to connect with her, simply send an email to info@redefiningsuccessstories.com and put Beth's name in the subject line.

THERE'S NO SUBSTITUTE
FOR HARD WORK

Orna Ben-Or Jackson

Whatever it is you want, get started today. Every step matters.

At an early age, my parents trusted me with the responsibility of caring for my younger brother and sister, which allowed me to do things on my own and fostered my independence. That independence became my guiding strength, and I work to actively pass that on to my own children today. I was born and raised in Israel, in a small town not far from Tel Aviv. My two younger siblings and I lived a happy and comfortable childhood in Israel with my parents. I found a love for sports and excelled in track and field, which built my confidence and taught me that I could accomplish anything I wanted with focused effort and dedication.

133

A few months after I became the Israeli high-jump champion at age 14, my parents told us we were moving to the United States. I was thrilled. It was the '80s and *Pretty in Pink* and *The Breakfast Club* had been huge international hits. I'd watched those movies several times and was enamored with the culture and lifestyle I saw portrayed. We moved to the United States because my dad wanted to be closer to his mom and two brothers who lived here. It's the shiny "land of opportunity" to Israelis, and my parents wanted to try their luck. It was much easier to get a working visa then, so they figured they had nothing to lose, packed up, and took the leap of faith.

My background in sports helped me assimilate into my new life in Fair Lawn, New Jersey. I joined the track and field team at school, which ended up being my ticket into the social scene. My English was limited, so my athletic ability made it much easier for me to feel like I belonged. I receive the second-place medal in Bergen County for the high jump, and placed sixth in the tristate area.

The hardest part of moving was the drastic change in finances that my family suddenly faced. My parents left behind respectable professional positions in Israel; my mom had been an assistant manager at a big bank and my dad had worked for Israel Aerospace Industries. Now that we'd moved, they both had to start from scratch. The upper-middle class lifestyle we enjoyed in Israel was gone. Suddenly we didn't have the basics as we'd moved with just a few suitcases and my parents didn't have jobs yet. For the first time in my life, we had to ask for help. I remember collecting tables, beds, nightstands, mattresses, and kitchenware from neighbors and good people who wanted to help.

It was my first experience with feeling "needy" and I didn't like it. I vowed then and there that I would never feel like that again. In Israel, my parents hadn't given me an allowance, but they always gave me money when I asked for it. After moving, I knew they didn't have the money they used to and I didn't want to ask them for it. I decided to stop relying on my parents and support myself financially as soon as I could, and went out to get a job and take care of my own needs. My fierce drive towards self-sufficiency and independence wasn't forced on me by my parents. They didn't expect me to work, but I was focused and determined to make sure I could provide for myself.

My first job as a teenager was at a local car wash. I worked as a cashier, every weekend from 7:00 a.m. to 5:00 p.m. I felt such pride at not having to ask my parents for anything. I remember buying my own clothes at local shops and feeling so accomplished and independent. I was disciplined about my spending and I saved most of the money I made. I loved the feeling of being able to buy what I wanted.

After graduating from high school I went to college, but only for one year. I quickly discovered that being a student wasn't appealing to me. I liked fashion, art, and photography. So I left school and decided to move to Manhattan.

Several months earlier, my dad had opened a clothing store on 7th Avenue, right in the heart of the clothing district in New York City. I started helping him in the store and I fell in love with the business and the work. After a few short months I told my dad that I wanted to take over the store. It had started as a small clothing store, where most items cost around $10, and we'd turned it into a boutique specializing in clubwear. As I grew into the position, I started by buying a few pieces of designer clothing and gradually proved my ability to spot the great finds that sold well, and I loved learning the trade.

After watching my hard work, dedication, and keen eye, my dad was so impressed that he gave me his blessing to take over and own the business. I was 19 years old. I withdrew the $12,000 that I'd saved by working at the car wash and invested it into the boutique. I was officially the owner. I had a little money left over, which I used to buy new merchandise and expand. I loved everything about the business. I created my own brand name "Manny's Closet," named after my brother.

I organized fashion shows at nightclubs and I hired 15 hairstylists, 15 makeup artists, and 30 models on a freelance basis for the fashion shows. It was so much fun! I would go out with my friends to the same clubs that hosted my shows and it was such a great feeling to have people recognize me and appreciate my work. I had three employees in the store and the business grew rapidly. But I was young, and my legitimacy as a storeowner would come in to question. Many sellers didn't believe that such a young woman could own and run a store, so I would carry a photo album with pictures of my clothing line, the fashion shows I conducted, and the store as a proof of my success. I remember saying things like, "This really is my store! I'm not lying!" I worked in the store for eight years, and grew the business, until I was 27 years old.

While I was running the store, I got married when I was 24 years old and had my first son, Ben, at 25 and my second son Daniel when I was 26 years old. My husband and I decided to move to New Jersey. After years of hard work at the boutique, the excitement and intense hours didn't work as well with my family, now that I was a mother. It took a while for me to accept that my two children meant that the store didn't fit my life anymore, but I knew it was time, and I shut down the store.

After staying home with the kids for a year, I knew that being a stay-at-home mom didn't suit me, and it was time to find my next adventure. I consulted my dad, who always gave me good advice, and we talked about the idea of real estate. My parents had become involved in real estate a few years earlier, so it was completely natural for me to choose this path. Later on, even my sister Hadas chose this field as well, and is still in the real estate business in New York City and Florida.

Real estate turned out to be a fabulous fit for me. I love meeting new people and talking to them, listening to their dreams, hopes, and ideals, and finding the best home for their needs. Choosing the right home is one of the biggest decisions most people make and it involves spouses and additional family members. It's not always an easy process. I truly enjoy making sure my clients are happy and comfortable with the entire experience. I'm filled with pride and happiness as I wake up every morning, get dressed to look and feel my best, and head out to and see my clients. Working in real estate requires hours outside the office and I prefer that to having a nine-to-five office job. My career has stretched from clothes to houses seamlessly because it's all about caring for my clients, and the sense of accomplishment I feel when they find the perfect fit.

As my new career in the world of real estate was beginning to take off, my marriage ended. I got divorced when my sons were four and five years old. It was challenging at first, especially because I wasn't known in the neighborhood and I didn't have a client base yet. Three of my close childhood friends generously lent me the money I needed to stand on my own two feet. I realize that having friends like that is not something to take for granted, and I will never forget that they were there for me at such a vulnerable time in my life. Over time, I paid them back every penny, and I will always be grateful. They were there for me mentally and financially, when I needed it the most and without conditions. Their example has taught me to always go the extra mile to help a friend in need.

When I started to work at Friedberg Properties, I was 27 years old. Marlyn Friedberg, my broker, and the branch manager Eleanor Stern introduced me to the business and taught me everything I needed to know. They mentored me, gave me confidence, and were like mothers to me. I attribute a great deal of my success to their guidance and I've worked to maintain a great relationship with them throughout the years. Deciding to leave Friedberg Properties after 12 years was incredibly difficult for me, and I can say it was almost traumatic for all of us. I'd experienced tremendous success with them and loyalty is important to me, so the decision wasn't made lightly. And it was a bit out of character for me. I still have the same accountant I used when I took over the boutique from my dad, I shop for my clothes in the same few stores, and I consistently go to the same restaurants. I like to joke that my accountant and the restaurants I dine in are the longest-term relationships I've had. So making the decision to leave Friedberg Properties to open up my own real estate group was scary for me. I was stepping far outside my comfort zone, but it was a move I had to make to continue the growth of my business and to create the work-life balance I wanted. So, I opened up the group with Sotheby's Prominent Properties, and named it the "Orna Jackson Group."

While I was working at Friedberg Properties, I met my second husband, Ezra. He was also divorced and had three children. We fell in love and decided to get married. We've added on to our family with two more amazing girls together who are loved by their big brothers and sister. It's been quite a journey, but we've created a unique family, and I relish the relationships and love that our blended family enjoys. Looking around our very full table during family dinners and holidays reminds me how fortunate I am.

My kids tell me I'm a "different" mom, because I don't tell them what to do. That's how I was raised, and it worked well for me, so I'm passing it on. I believe that the best way to teach children that there's nothing they can't achieve is to set an example. I always tell my kids to do what feels right for them and to be kind to others. I'm aware that they're watching me, and I'm proud of what they're seeing. I've made a conscious effort to be involved in their schools and to donate my time and money where needed. My kids know that I work hard, and they see the rewards of that hard work, and I hope they take that work ethic to college, even though they tease me about not graduating myself.

As my own career has taken off and my family has grown, I've turned towards helping my community. I got involved in the Jewish and Israeli community as a member of Lubavitch on the Palisades and the Palisades Business Network where we meet once a month and discuss business challenges and how members of the group can help each other with their contacts. Then, a few years ago, I established a support group for the families who've relocated to the United States. As someone who's been through it, I can completely empathize with the challenges and fears that come from such a big move. I wanted to put my experience to use and help these families, especially the women coming here. Many of the women in this support group have moved here because their husbands were relocated for work, and they end up staying at home with their children while their spouses are busy working and establishing their careers. The burden and stress of relocation falls on them, in addition to the day-to-day changes, confusion, and loneliness that are natural when moving to a new country. I get to know these women during a tough time in their lives and it brings me incredible joy to be there for them.

After working with these families, I wanted to figure out a way to bring them into the established community here. I started organizing monthly breakfast meetings so the women in our community could come together and meet new friends. We make sure to include a mix of families at each breakfast: those who've just moved here, and those who've been here for years. I'm happy to report that it's become wildly successful. I find it heartwarming and inspiring to see people open up and discuss their challenges and watch the community respond with open arms and support. Because the breakfasts were so successful, I started a WhatsApp group for Israeli women, and we have about 100 active members. Anyone can post a question or ask for help, and they'll receive immediate feedback or a helpful contact.

Whenever a new family comes to the area I let the group know how many kids they have, what ages they are, and where they're going to live. I also introduce them to my favorite Jewish schools and temples in the area to provide a feeling of home and tradition. The other members reach out to each other and help that family settle in. It's so comforting and rewarding to know that I've been part of something that makes a difference for families that are in the same position my family was in all those years ago. I love connecting these new families to established families in the community, as I've always had a strong instinct for knowing which people need to be introduced to each other. While listening to people is part of my job, I don't just listen to be polite. I find that I'm always listening for how I can help them by introducing them to the right people. I remember how hard it was for my parents and for our whole family and know the value of having a friend to listen and help.

I would define success as truly knowing yourself and understanding what you need to be happy in life. It's not always about the path that everyone else wants us to take, or the path we're "supposed" to take. If I had lived my life that way, I might have finished four years of college and become an accountant or something, but I would have missed out on all of the opportunities and adventures that have made me who I am. The real win in life for me has been doing what I love to do, doing it with confidence, and making a difference while financially supporting my family and strengthening my community.

When I reflect back on the path I've chosen, I don't regret anything. Even leaving college early was the right choice for me and I've never let it hold me back. As long as we're reaching out and helping as many people as we can on our individual paths to success, it's impossible to fail.

I know that anything is possible through hard work, dedication and determination. If you have those ingredients, there are no boundaries for what you can achieve, even if you have to carry around a photo album with you to prove how *successful you really are.*

A note from Sarah and Ally: Orna has something in common with most of the authors in the book: starting work at a very young age, and working through anything that life can dish out. We love that she started her journey through her careers by working in a car wash and saving almost every penny. There are some of us who learned discipline and responsibility early on, and kept it. Orna is a shining example of what's possible when we apply the best of who we are, no matter what work we're doing.

We've been told by the "gurus" that the best thing you can do to move yourself forward is to get started right now, today, and do the best with what you have. Kind of like the old adage, "Be the best hamburger flipper" which was popular during the last generation. But how much moxie does it take to do your best when those you're working with don't even believe that you're capable of doing what you're doing? We loved that Orna didn't let that stop her, and instead, she solved the problem by carrying around a photo album. Brilliant. One other thing we hope you take away from Orna's story: once you've reached a level of success that makes you happy, pay it forward. Learn how to share with your community and connect other people. Show how much you care by being there for others when times are hard for them, too. A rising tide lifts all boats, and pulling others up when they need us is a vital aspect of true and lasting success.

Chapter Challenge

What part of Orna's story could you relate to the most?

_____

_____

If you could name only one thing you took away from this story, what would it be?

_____

_____

_____

What one thing will you do differently because of Orna's story?

_____

_____

What surprised you the most in this story?

_____

_____

If there was one thing you could ask Orna, what would it be?

_____

_____

We'd love for you to connect with Orna. If you'd like to connect with her, simply send an email to info@redefiningsuccessstories.com and put Orna's name in the subject line.

WHEN LIFE HAPPENS, SAY YES

Kerri Kimball

More often than not, what we really need finds us.

I grew up in a traditional suburban home in the San Francisco Bay Area in the roaring consumerism of the '70s and '80s. We lived through water rationing, gas rationing, we didn't wear seat belts, and we moved into a brand-new tract house when I was almost five. We went to church every Sunday and our friends were the families who sat next to us on the front pews. We were a close-knit Mormon congregation and we helped each other and celebrated births, weddings, and funerals.

My parents were barely able to cover the mortgage payment, put food on the table and clothes on their four fast-growing children. We never went to the doctor unless we needed stitches or had broken bones. But every once in a while a new prize would appear in our home: a stereo, a microwave, or a new sofa. It was made clear to us that this was the result of saving up and finding a good deal at the store. We treated the new asset with great care and respect. It was a great education in respecting money.

As the oldest, I was my dad's helper and even worked at his office from time to time, which made me feel special as his attention was a prized commodity. He would talk to me about his tax business and real estate investments. I listened carefully, and I understood. When I was eight, my parents started a company called KTD Enterprises, our own little family company, and they made me president. We worked odd jobs and deposited the money into an account to save for a trip to Disneyland. I remember endorsing checks to the account when I had barely learned to write my name in cursive.

I was bright, albeit unfocused. I loved school, I loved to read and I got good grades, and tested well on college entrance exams. My friends were applying to California state schools and that sounded a whole lot more fun than Brigham Young University (BYU). My secret non-Mormon boyfriend also liked the idea of my staying close by. But a two-year full-ride scholarship to BYU, combined with the fear of disobeying my parents, meant that at the end of summer 1987 I was one of the 4,854 freshmen attending BYU in Provo, Utah.

This is when the pressure to get married started to mount. I was encouraged to marry young and start a family right away. My fellow female students and I were there to get a college degree so we would have a fallback plan in case something happened to our future husbands. Doubts started to tug at me, and I couldn't make sense of the expectations laid at my feet. When did my fertility become more important than my brain? Why did being smart and good at business stop being important qualities at age 18? It was a long four years of progressive disenchantment with Mormonism and the lifestyle it prescribed for me as a woman. By graduation I was determined to break away, even if my family rejected me. I wrote a bold five-page letter to my parents denouncing my membership in their church, and then stayed out of contact with them for several years.

I graduated into a recession and didn't immediately land my dream job in finance. I moved to Park City, Utah, to live with a boyfriend and wait tables. We scraped together enough money to fly to Seville, Spain, where a friend got us jobs at the World Expo. We bounced around southern Spain, Portugal, and Morocco and he surfed while I read on the beach. When funds and friends ran out, we returned to the U.S. and spent more months waiting tables.

We eventually broke up and I found my way to San Francisco in 1993, which is where I got my first job making $21,000 a year with no benefits. Finally! Financial stability and pride in my work. Life revolved around friends and we commiserated about the trials of entry-level work over cheap bottles of wine and pasta dinners. I was adrift in my dating life, having breached the security barrier of marrying before graduating BYU. I was ill-equipped to set my own boundaries, they had always been given to me and closely enforced through the rigors of religion. Fortunately work kept going well and I learned the ins and outs of the financial management of advertising agencies.

I met an amazing young man, Tom, at work and we fell in love. An opportunity came up to transfer to an agency in Sydney, Australia, and we both jumped at it. Sydney offered more responsibility over smaller budgets and proved to be a great résumé-builder. We worked hard and saved our money, and after two years we gave notice and took an unforgettable one-year traveling sabbatical. We drove the circumference of Australia and then New Zealand in a four-wheeler, explored the dusty back roads of Southeast Asia with locals, and trekked the ancient trails of Nepal. I spent my 31st birthday in Gokyo, a tiny village near Everest Base Camp. I was, literally, on the top of the world.

We had three more months of extraordinary travel in India and northern Europe, and then landed back in the United States. We drove across the country, looking like hippies with our woven necklaces, yak hair sweaters, and relaxed faces. Our country had changed while we were gone; the tech bubble had grown and burst, everyone drank from water bottles, and all the ads had a .com in them. We landed in New York, and the sprawl of the city was suffocating after our travels. But even as the diversity of the East Village was comforting, our relationship didn't survive the adjustment.

After we broke up, I'd learned enough about myself to know that I'd have to reconcile some things before I could have a healthy, balanced life. Breaking with religion and family was the easy part, the hard part was reconciling. I refused to feel guilty, but I missed the feeling of belonging. I'd learned that the Mormon Church wasn't necessarily my problem and I needed to look deeper. I knew it was time to take responsibility for my own choices. There were some hard conversations with my parents and siblings, and I made some long-overdue apologies. Studying transformational technologies, I sat in class after class and watched a lot of unhappy women shed their old problems and come to life when serving their true purpose and passion. I realized that there are a variety of ways women are disempowered, not just through religion. As I grew to own my power, it dawned on me that I could create a career that would really matter to me.

Around this time I met with a friend's financial advisor. Although I'd earned a good salary I had lived beyond my means. The advisor showed me how to consolidate and rebalance my accounts. He pointed out that Tom was still the named beneficiary of my retirement savings. The process of working with him was empowering. I thought, "I'm a finance person, why not work in financial services?" His firm was hiring and I knew a senior advisor at the firm who promised to mentor me and help me to be a success, so I applied for the job.

I failed hard and I failed fast. It turns out, this was a totally different world and I had signed on for a thinly veiled eat-what-you-kill sales job. They paid a stipend but not enough to avoid raiding my retirement accounts to make ends meet. My strong suits failed me. The skills I'd learned in corporate life were irrelevant and building relationships with the all-male leaders in the organization made me well-liked but didn't bring in any clients. I was truly on my own with my very slim Rolodex, everyone I knew was 3,000 miles away.

I cried every day. I cried to everyone who would listen. At a visceral level, something was wrong. I'd learned early on that hard work and following the rules meant fair compensation. I was miserable without the paycheck and the sense of approval that went with it. They should have fired me early on. The only reason they didn't is because they needed women on the team to look diverse.

I kept up appearances and practiced on my friends. I learned to network. I networked my ass off from 7:00 in the morning until 9:00 at night. I learned to ask for referrals. I learned to call and talk people into meeting with me. I got one client. Then another client. I studied for and passed the series 7, 63, and 65. My colleagues made fun of me for getting a score of 92 on the series 7. Apparently you're only supposed to study enough to pass it, not to get an A. I focused on working with women, delivering the experience of freedom and power over their finances, and I got a few more clients. The joy of those moments kept me going. So did my stubborn reluctance to admit I'd made a mistake. Little by little the elements of my dream job came together as I went to fun events to network and talk to people about my services. I hosted financial salons at clients' homes. I joined women's groups.

At one event I met a chic woman who was starting a firm with all women advisors. I interviewed on my 38th birthday and got the job. When I submitted my resignation to the managing partner of my current firm he didn't try to talk me into staying but he warned "putting a skirt on it isn't going to make it any different." The all-women firm was a healthier environment and I was hungry for women mentors, women who had experienced some of the same fears and hurdles I had, and found success. I learned everything I could.

Then the financial crisis hit. Going to the office every day was nerve-wracking and the unimaginable kept happening. But I didn't lose any clients. In fact, that year my client base grew, and grew quickly. People suddenly felt the need for professional financial advice, and I was proud of what we were offering. There were a few months where I made enough money to contribute to my own retirement savings for the first time in four years.

As the economy began to find solid ground, I hit 40 and launched into personal crisis. Dating in my late 30s had been spectacularly unsuccessful and my window to have children was closing. I began a treatment course to freeze my embryos. Rigorous hormone shots led to an emotional roller coaster. Shopping online for a sperm donor was a new low. I seriously considered tricking good friends into "accidentally" getting me pregnant. Ultimately the procedure was a failure and no embryos were healthy enough to freeze. I was at rock bottom and had no plans for Thanksgiving. A friend suggested we go to a yoga retreat in the Catskills. It sounded better than eating a turkey burger alone.

During a vegetarian meal on the ashram floor, I met an interesting Chilean man named Jorge, who worked at the United Nations. I noticed that he showed up for sunrise meditation and didn't complain about karma yoga chores. He was intelligent and charming. When we got back to the city, we met for lunches, then dinners, and friendship grew into love. I was up-front about wanting to try to have children, although my hopes were low. He had two accomplished grown daughters but was open to having more children. He was everything I had asked the universe for. The next year we got engaged and moved in together.

Sensitive to the passing months, I started a fertility diet and agreed with Jorge that we'd start trying to get pregnant while we were engaged. It took one month. We were elated and decided to marry before the baby came. We quickly threw together a small destination wedding in beautiful Marin County, California. I was nervous about telling my family that I was having a shotgun wedding but they were so gracious and happy for us, they didn't give me a hard time.

Baby Benjamin arrived that summer and I took three months of maternity leave, then hired a full-time nanny and went back to work. During my leave, cracks had started to show at the office. They had let go the newer advisors and moved the office to a residential neighborhood. The compensation structure changed and resources were slowly being stripped away. It became harder and harder to provide the service my clients had come to expect.

One other advisor remained and we began to bond over shared complaints. We both tried to negotiate better conditions with management but were unsuccessful. We started to talk about alternatives. We had strong client relationships and no non-compete with our current firm. If we combined our businesses, we were big enough to open a new company. We could deliver our clients independent, world-class fiduciary advice and concierge service. The concept behind Apogee Wealth Advisors was born.

The two of us spent a year quietly interviewing independent broker-dealers, drinking from the fire hose of compensation packages, cost structures, payouts, platforms, resources, and IT. We talked with countless other advisors. We asked accountants and attorneys for advice on how to set up our company properly. During that year I completed my CERTIFIED FINANCIAL PLANNER™ certification, studying on vacation and after hours while my husband watched the baby. After that I studied and passed the Series 24 exam to become office supervisor so we could earn a higher payout.

I had butterflies the size of eagles the morning we resigned March 11, 2013. We both arrived early at the office that Monday morning, met with the partners, and submitted our resignations. They somehow hadn't caught wind of our plans and were caught by surprise. We expressed gratitude for all we had learned and declined their offer to negotiate. We walked out the door, hopped into a cab, and by the time we arrived at our new offices at 477 Madison Ave., our licenses had transferred and Apogee Wealth Advisors was in business. We began calling clients to let them know about the change, and in the end all but two clients came with us.

The first few months were chaotic as we processed transfer paperwork, set up systems, brought staff on board, and got our IT up and running. In that first year my income doubled. As more interesting and successful women heard about Apogee and became clients, the experience of helping them organize their financial worlds and meet their goals didn't feel like empowerment, because these women already owned their power. This was teamwork.

These women demanded the opportunity to make a difference with their investment dollars through values-based investing. Some were very uncomfortable with the portfolios they had inherited, full of companies that were harming the environment or conducting animal testing. I was able to offer conscious investments that generated results comparable to standard portfolios. It was fun, and lucrative, to create portfolios based on global impact, not just financial performance.

Jorge and I held out hope for having another baby but I'd wanted the firm to launch before trying again. We had just moved our family to the suburbs and a friend introduced me to a wonderful local holistic women's health center. I studied natural conception and ate whole foods. At the age of 44, I conceived after three months of trying.

Baby Adrian came a week before his due date after a five-hour un-medicated labor that went so fast the midwife didn't make it to the hospital in time. This time I asked my mom and dad to come and stay with us for a month after the baby came. After they left my two sisters came for a week. I wanted to share the special tiny newborn weeks with family and to have them feel close to my children. After all we'd been through, this intimacy and caring was a dream come true. I had followed my instincts and hadn't lost my family.

It would have been wonderful if the journey had been a straight line to success. I ignored a lot of great advice that would have made life easier. But I had to take risks and learn from my own mistakes. The greatest surprise is how much I love being a mother. My boys are my biggest source of joy. I came darn close to not having kids at all and I'm pretty sure if motherhood had come easier and earlier, I wouldn't enjoy it as much.

I love to think what life will be like in five years. My boys will need me less and their worlds outside the home will be more exciting. My house will be in less dire need of renovations. I'll be 50 and traveling again. The clients I serve will have grown more successful and my staff will have developed and achieved dreams of their own. The shape of financial advice will certainly have changed with the fast pace of technology and we'll be running to keep one step ahead. We'll be closer to the day when it doesn't make sense to make a distinction between male and female clients, or between male and female employees. We'll all be able to ask for and receive the things we need. To set a goal and to achieve that goal without anyone else putting barriers in the way.

A note from Sarah and Ally: After reading Kerri's story, we felt this lovely feeling of peace and ease. When Kerri decided to do something, she made it happen. While some of her decisions were difficult and trying (harvesting eggs is not for the weak of heart), she always grabbed the tools that were offered to her, and made the most of the connections with those around her.

How many of us would have given up when faced with a job that wasn't what we thought? It's so much easier to shrug our shoulders and make someone else out to be the bad guy as we skate off into another job or position that we already know how to do, or one that doesn't challenge us the way we deserve. Kerri dug in her heels, listened to the calling, and created an entire career path for herself. Not something everyone would have chosen to do, and it really paid off.

And while she was digging in her heels, she also stayed alert and receptive to the "magic" that life can offer at times. She said yes to an all-woman firm (despite a comment about skirts from her male boss, ahem), she said yes to her new business partner, and she said yes to that retreat with her friend. Finally, she said yes to having children after 40 by doing everything within her power to take care of her body and surroundings. Hard work will always be required for those of us who really want to succeed, but we don't have to do it alone. When we say yes to the opportunities placed before us, we create the environment for optimal results.

Chapter Challenge

What part of Kerri's story could you relate to the most?

_____

_____

If you could name only one thing you took away from this story, what would it be?

_____

_____

_____

What one thing will you do differently because of Kerri's story?

_____

_____

What surprised you the most in this story?

_____

_____

_____

If there was one thing you could ask Kerri, what would it be?

_____

_____

We'd love for you to connect with Kerri. If you'd like to connect with her, simply send an email to info@redefiningsuccessstories.com and put Kerri's name in the subject line.

NEVER LOSE YOURSELF

Gretchen Lolis

People love to share their opinions about what you need to do to get ahead. But if they suggest compromising who you are, walk away and stay true to yourself.

There's been one mantra that's powered me through my career in fashion, "You have to look good, to feel good, to do good." Not exactly something I thought about very much as I was growing up in Iowa. Well, maybe the part about looking good, I've always liked that part. But as I've climbed my way up the fashion ladder, the mantra has morphed a little bit. It's become, "Do good, to feel good, to look good." It's changed because even when you're at the top of your game, you need to leave room to grow, and that's starts with the "doing." I realized that one morning not long ago, as I sat at my

163

desk, having reached one of my biggest lifelong goals. I'd become the VP of sales at my company, but I felt unfulfilled, restless and I found myself asking, "Is this all there is?"

The answer, of course, is that it's up to us to decide. We can settle and think we're done, shouting, "Mission accomplished!" and then wonder why we don't feel great. Or we can stare into the abyss of "is this all there is?" and declare something new, something more, and strengthen ourselves each moment along the way.

The first time I heard my mantra, it was 1992 at a fashion show in South Carolina. As the event was getting underway, a minister walked up to the microphone to begin his opening remarks. I'm not sure how a minister at a fashion event was able to articulate the passion I have for my work so well, but he did. And while it came from an unlikely source, I felt a thrill run through my whole body as he said the words:

"You have to look good, to feel good, to do good."

That was it! That was why I loved my job so much! I had fallen in love with the idea that I could make any woman, any age, any size, any color, feel amazing if I could get her in the right clothes. And I knew that if I could make her feel good she would be happy, and happy people make other people happy, too. I knew I loved clothes and fashion, but this gave me the deeper meaning behind that love.

The clothes are great, but only if they do their job. They have to make a woman feel good.

But let me take you back a little bit and give you the whole story. I'm a worker. I've always been a worker. I got my work ethic from my parents. They're true entrepreneurs and throughout my life, they've worked through several new businesses until they found their passion and true calling in real estate. Using my mom's business savvy and my dad's moxie, they've built and grown their business into the largest real estate agency in the Iowa Great Lakes Region. They built a brand before "building a brand" was trendy. I grew up watching their grit, integrity, and perseverance, and I chose to follow their example. That drive supported me through most of my career, and I'm very proud of that.

As with most careers, and lives, it's been a series of ups and downs. I've had people around me that build me up, and some that have tried to knock me down. A quick piece of advice: Steer clear of the knocker-downers. They're not fun, and there's no reason to be around them. Look around at the people you work with and find the good ones. And that includes the janitor, the people who clean the office, the mailroom workers, receptionists, and assistants. Good people are everywhere, but it's up to us to find them.

It's the good people who've helped me get where I am without losing my personality or breaking my spirit. I wasn't born in New York City, nor did I have an easy ticket into the world of fashion. Quite the opposite, actually. I graduated from high school in Arnolds Park, Iowa, with a whopping 18 kids in my graduating class. Then I went to Iowa State University, much to the surprise of my high school guidance counselor who told my parents that Iowa State was too big and competitive and I would never make it. Nice, right? She was a knocker-downer. I've never given them much credence.

About six months before I was scheduled to graduate (take *that,* guidance counselor!) I landed my first job in fashion, an internship at Liz Claiborne. I was on a study tour in New York City during March Market, which is an event for buyers to come from all over the country to New York to buy clothes for their stores. The specialty store I was working for in Iowa had traveled to the market and I joined them in the Liz Claiborne showroom. While we were there, the powerhouse couple I was working for told the senior vice president of sales at Liz Claiborne that I was looking for a summer internship. He asked for my résumé.

While I felt a little trickle of excitement, I was still nervous. I was "just a girl from Iowa" and I didn't think New York City was that great. So I didn't really plan on turning my résumé into that senior vice president. I made my way back to the Howard Johnson Hotel on 51st Street and 8th Avenue in Hell's Kitchen, before Hell's

Kitchen was cool, and called my parents. I casually mentioned the conversation in the showroom and they both said, "You have to do it!" I can still hear my father's voice insisting, "Send in your résumé! You can do anything for eight weeks!"

My parents were always my biggest fans and supporters, and their belief in me carried me during moments when I didn't believe. They saw this opportunity at Liz Claiborne, and they knew I had to take it. Their support gave me the courage I needed. They promised me that along with the internship came a one-way ticket home in case I needed it. They pushed me to get out there and do my best, while providing a safe place for me to land. It's something I've never taken for granted. Life has always been good to me, starting with giving me parents like mine.

I've always loved clothes. I love putting them together, and seeing which pieces work best with others. But there was one moment of understanding that stands out from all the others. During one of my breaks in college, my mom had picked me up; while we were driving home she started to share how down she was feeling lately. My mom was a size 18 and it wasn't easy to find clothes that she felt good wearing. Right then and there I told her to drive us straight to a specialty shop I knew. We spent hours in the store that day, trying on new clothes, playing with different tops and bottoms and we found my mom a whole new wardrobe! There was and still is a very profound joy that filled me up that day. I had become my mom's "personal shopper." *My* mom, the woman who had always given me so much love and support. I felt like I had found a small way to pay her back for everything she'd done for me. And I also found a new desire to make other women feel that way, too. As many women as I could find.

As luck would have it, my first sales job at Liz Claiborne was in a brand-new division, Elisabeth, their plus-size line. We were pioneers in the market and I got to travel the country giving fashion shows and seminars. Given the experience with my mom, this was incredibly personal for me. I was making a difference helping these women and they were so thankful and sincere. I knew that my work mattered. My belief in that minister's words grew stronger.

My love of fashion was growing and I was eager to move up the ladder as fast as I could. I worked hard to make sure everyone I worked with could rely on me, and I was quick to get the work done. If that meant I couldn't step out for lunch that day I would eat at my desk. I did what it took to get the job done, and I always had my eye on the next level. Early on in my career, being the bold "go-get-'em" type that I am, I told the president of my division that I wanted more accounts, more money, a promotion, and most importantly, more respect. She looked at me as if looking at an impetuous child and said, "Oh, Gretchen, it takes more than being cute, fun, nice, and bubbly to be promoted."

My ego was shredded. I held it together, but I knew I could conquer the fashion world and prove the president of my division wrong. It was time to get the experience I needed, but I was determined to do it without losing my personality and traits that make me unique. I didn't want to turn into a hard-edged woman; I didn't have to be cranky and dull just to get ahead. My talent, keen eye for trends, and my tenacity were going to carry me to the top, with my personality intact. With laser-like focus, I forged ahead. I learned how to crunch numbers faster than anyone else. I could calculate margins, percentages, and the number of pieces needed in my head, and with precision. My Iowan naiveté served me well because I was afraid of nothing! I knew that my parents had worked hard and succeeded, so I could do the same.

Throughout my career I would talk to everyone in my line of sight: the janitors, the men and women in the mailroom, the receptionists, and those above me. As a junior account executive, I would say hi to the "big shots" in my industry. No one was safe from a cheerful handshake and a "Hi! I'm Gretchen." And that includes Calvin Klein. When I was working there, we were told not to talk to him, or ask him questions. But rules aside, when he and I shared an elevator one morning, I made sure to say, "Good morning." And of course he smiled. I have a feeling in his head he was thinking, "Ah! A rule-breaker." I attribute my success in this industry to my belief that we're all human. Job titles and prestige don't mean anything at the end of the day. We're all human, we're all the same, and everyone deserves to hear "Good morning" in an elevator, even Calvin Klein.

My cheerful determination served me well as my career in fashion progressed. My genuine connections with people ended up creating my career path for me. Because I was so focused, quick with numbers, and fast on the job, the people I'd created connections with loved working with me. I've never once looked for a job. Work has always found me because people have asked me to come and work with them. I'm so proud of that. And it is proof to me that while I've made it in one of the most cutthroat and challenging industries out there, I've stayed true to who I really am. I love people, and I love my work. I earned those phone calls and invitations to work, and I did it all while remaining "cute, fun, nice, and bubbly."

All of this leads me back to the beginning of my story when I was wondering if all of that hard work and ladder climbing was worth it. I had been working for my current company for almost two years and business wasn't going well. My job security was at an all-time low, and I knew that I could be let go at any minute. It's not easy to be your best when you don't feel secure. The real pressure was there for me because this job provides health care and financial stability for my family. I sat there feeling alone, insecure, scared, and defeated. I would randomly burst into tears. I was depressed and just not myself. I was in this terrified daze for weeks.

Then something inside me started to light up. I realized that I had faced hard times before and I'd made it through just fine. In fact, more often than not, I came out stronger. I knew I had to "look in the mirror and make a change" to quote my favorite song. (Miss you, Michael!) I've had the thrill of working for some of the biggest fashion brands on 7th Avenue: Liz Claiborne, Jones New York, and Calvin Klein Jeans. I have had the pleasure of being the vice president of sales for Silver Jeans since 2012, which was a goal I set in January of 1990 when I moved to New York City. Getting here was tough, and I worked like a madwoman, staying true to myself the entire time. In addition to the hard work, I have sacrificed, experienced setbacks, fun, madness, growth, learning, sharing, tears, and pride.

While I was in my daze, my feelings about my job grew more complicated. I felt lucky to be there and have the experience, even as I was petrified about the future. Through my years in sales, I've met amazing people and had the honor to mentor dozens of brilliant women. It's been a wonderful journey. And while I was grateful for my position, I knew there was more for me out there. I had reached the top, but it wasn't enough. Managing my own expectations, and owning that I wasn't satisfied was a challenge for me. I knew I wanted to keep my job as VP of sales because I love it, I'm confident in it, and I like helping my company make money. But as I sat there at my desk wondering what had happened, I realized that there was more for me to do.

Twenty years ago I read the John Irving book *Cider House Rules* while I was on a business trip. There is one line in the book that's stayed with me, "Everyone needs someone to believe in them." I know this is true, and I revel in the fact that I've always had people cheering for me. I've had incredible luck and good fortune. And I feel compelled to pay that forward. I want to find ways to support anyone that might need it. To date, my work has given that gift to me. I love making women feel supported and to let them know they have someone cheering them on, too. I believe in the power of kind words, a great outfit, and a shoulder to lean on.

My advice to all of us is to be the very best at everything we do, even if what we're doing isn't our end game. We always look up to the best in every position, mailroom clerk, housekeeper, administrative assistant, sales person, vice president, CEO. There has to be someone who is the best at every job, and it's up to us to be that person. When we work hard to be the best, our eyes will always have that special glint of pride mixed with a little bit of mischievousness. And that little twinkle in our eye makes us feel good. And you know what I believe: When you feel good, you *do* good, and you will look good! It really works in any order, so I say we start with the inside when it comes to our work.

So I used this rough patch in my career to dig even deeper and become even better. Our numbers have turned around and I know I'm even better at my job now. It took me a year of insecurity and looking over my shoulder to figure out that I'm right where I should be. This last year was a time for me to stretch and grow, filled with emotions that I had to deal with and lots of hard questions that I had to answer. And what I've learned from this year is that these moments will continue to happen as long as we're pushing our own limits, because after all the hard work, good luck and success, if we're not growing, we're shrinking. So tough times are part of that, big deal. With a little tenacity and grit, we get through them. And once we decide to let them in, they usually serve us.

My mantra has proven itself. I've built great friendships, made professional connections, and have been given opportunities that I could have never imagined. I believe in my mantra because I've worked to be nice, enthusiastic, and, yes bubbly, while putting in the hard work that's necessary for lasting success.

A note from Sarah and Ally: How many women could make it through the cutthroat industry of fashion with such fun, grace, and authenticity? We feel so honored to have both Neepa and Gretchen

173

as examples for women who love fashion, but who may not be willing to head into the industry because of its bad, The Devil Wears Prada reputation. But Gretchen's story is living proof that you can make it all the way to the top, and even help a start-up thrive, when you stay true to who you really are.

Gretchen is one of those women that lights up a room when she walks in. And not just because she's "cute, fun, nice, and bubbly." She brings such genuine warmth and caring into every interaction she has, which makes her a magnet for all that's good and supportive. As she says in her story, "We all need someone to believe in us," and Gretchen makes sure she is that person for those in her life. You can feel that come through in her story as well.

As we move through our day-to-day, it's important to remember what Gretchen said about being kind to everyone in her surroundings. We found out after she wrote her chapter that the people from the mailroom and housekeeping at her office were invited to her daughter's christening. There are no titles, boundaries, or differences for the people in Gretchen's life. Everyone she connects with receives her love and attention. She lives that, and there's no question that has contributed to her success.

174

Chapter Challenge

What part of Gretchen's story could you relate to the most?

_____

_____

If you could name only one thing you took away from this story, what would it be?

_____

_____

_____

What one thing will you do differently because of Gretchen's story?

_____

_____

What surprised you the most in this story?

_____

_____

_____

If there was one thing you could ask Gretchen, what would it be?

_____

_____

We'd love for you to connect with Gretchen. If you'd like to connect with her, simply send an email to info@redefiningsuccessstories.com and put Gretchen's name in the subject line.

BE OPEN TO CHANGE

Melanie Catanzaro

Every new chapter in life can bring surprises and gifts, but it's up to us to leverage them.

My life has been a series of highs and lows as I've ventured through different phases. During one of the higher points, I was the only human being riding in the back of a FedEx cargo plane headed for Japan. My companions on the flight included dozens of birds, collectible cars, thousands of crates, and contemporary art worth over $200 million. That art was why I was on the plane. I was responsible for it. I remember anxiously shifting back and forth in my seat, with *Japanese for Dummies* chanting through my earphones, and I couldn't wait to see Tokyo. The pilots let me sit in the cockpit on the way up the runway, which was such a rush, but for the rest of the flight I had to sit in the back and watch that art. I was a very confident 25-year-old in my third year of working for Sotheby's in New York City. But confidence aside, I still had knots in my stomach. It was my second trip overseas with a traveling exhibition of artwork, but this was my first trip to a non-English speaking country. On my first trip I had the pleasure of traveling on a FedEx cargo plane to London. I remember being terrified to be alone outside of my home country, but I had quickly caught the travel bug.

After spending a few years working for Sotheby's guarding and transporting some of the most valuable art in the world, I decide to go back to graduate school at night for my MBA at New York University. I'd been given so much responsibility so quickly and I wanted to be the best I could be. There were people lining up for my job at the prestigious auction house, and I knew there was no room for mistakes. By going back to school, I could acquire the skills and competencies that would make me the most successful in my work. I wanted to be so great that no one would notice that I was a young manager. But after two years of going to school at night, I couldn't keep up with the travel and the schoolwork. I asked for a leave of absence so I could finish my last year full-time. I was paying for school and I wanted the effort, and the student loans, to be worth it.

I had every intention of going back to Sotheby's after I got my degree. But during the first full-time semester at school, I was encouraged by classmates and professors to participate in on-campus recruiting and career fairs. I quickly realized the overwhelming amount of career opportunities out there and I started to push myself even harder. I knew that these new possibilities would mean leaving the comforts of my former job, which I loved, but I wanted to pursue them.

Later that year during spring break, I traveled to Russia with ten friends from business school. Living on the edge had never been my mantra but I remember catching a glimpse of my shadow as I hung onto the train car handle. In the light of the White Nights, the wind was whipping through my hair in as we sped through the Russian countryside at over 100 miles per hour. I felt very edgy indeed. I was riding, definitely not sleeping, on the overnight train from Moscow to St. Petersburg. I was 28 years old at this point, and an upcoming graduate from NYU Stern School of Business with a great job lined up for the following September at Unilever. At that moment in time, I think I was bolder than I had ever been. I was confident that I could conquer Russia and then, the rest of the world. Experiencing this egotistical, arrogant, hard-as-nails country fit right into my mindset at the time. After working at Sotheby's, going to school at night, and landing a new high-paying job, I was feeling incredibly accomplished. I was more than ready for the next part of my life to begin, and to kick ass in every part of it.

I continued to nurture my travel bug, and four months later, during the summer after I got my degree, I was standing at the highest mountain pass in India, walking around as if I was on the moon at over 17,000 feet above sea level at Tanglang La. There was so little oxygen that I felt like the wind had been knocked out of me just by walking around taking pictures. I'd spent the previous month in India and Nepal with a good friend from business school, and we'd experienced the culture with local Indians who had been born into a higher caste. We had seen the best these countries have to offer, from the gorgeous dynamic landscape, to the amazing cities of Delhi, Mumbai and Katmandu, to Annapurna and the Taj Mahal.

On the streets of India we witnessed the worst of life circumstances as we faced the realities of true poverty. The masses living on the streets, making do with the few things they possessed. The children were dirty and skinny, but they were smiling and playing happily in the streets. All the arrogance I had felt only months before faded away. That poverty had a profound impact on my perspective, and my future. I wanted to work hard, be successful, and earn money, but I wanted to balance all of that with what I could do for others.

I returned from that trip a new person. I was grounded by the realities

I had seen. I was still passionate about the future, but with a new mindset of gratitude, a dedication to hard work, and a renewed energy about being a good person along the way. Without that, all of the hard work and money didn't matter. Something happened to me during that summer of travel. Coming back home after seeing how other people live around the world, I set out to build the rest of my career and personal life with passion and drive, but with much more humility.

I didn't have a childhood filled with overseas vacations, so these trips didn't come naturally. I grew up in the '70s as a daughter of conservative, Catholic parents who never traveled outside the United States. My father was a civil servant in law enforcement his entire life. My mother returned to work when I was four. I thought having a working mom was very cool, and I enjoyed playing office while she was working at the medical practice she managed. As an office manager, she was able to participate in several aspects of the business, and she would carefully explain each one to me. We had no help at home other than my aging grandmother across the street, so the office was a much better indoor playground for me. I loved every minute of helping her answer phones and greeting patients. Both my mom and the doctor she worked for were extremely open to my help. I continued to work for them throughout my teenage years and into college. My mother was always incredibly hard-working, confident, and proud. I wanted to be just like her when I grew up.

My older sister was another source of influence. She's eight years older than me and I eagerly watched her when she got her first job out of college at a law firm. She left for work every day in beautiful suits and heels, and I was so proud, and a little bit jealous. Today she's a working mother of three amazing girls between the ages of 26 and 16. She and her supportive husband balance their own careers while raising these incredible young women to be self-sufficient, driven, and committed to experiencing the world. I still look to my sister as an example as I raise my own children.

Throughout my professional life, I've also watched the different women I've worked for, and I've noticed they have similar traits. From my first days at Sotheby's to my many years at Unilever, these women were all driven to excel in their careers, passionate about their work, and committed to developing strong teams. They broke glass ceilings and worked hard to prove themselves. I've worked for many childless women who've dedicated their lives and careers to breaking down barriers in top companies. I've also worked for women who had children and watched them forfeit time with their families to move up the corporate ladder. While I admired the courage, persistence, and tenacity of all of these women, the more senior I became, the less willing I was to make certain sacrifices.

As a mother of three children, a daughter and a set of identical twin boys, I've always been determined to find that special mix of a meaningful career and being an involved, hands-on parent. In the corporate world I struggled with the many overseas trips and long hours, which left little time for my children, my husband, or myself. I tried flexible work arrangements and even attempted a short stint as a part-time director, but it wasn't sustainable as a department head. Senior management was looking for my full participation on a daily basis, and it didn't work.

After business school, I spent 13 years working for an international company, but ultimately I decided to go out and start my own business. My job was changing and I knew this was the opportunity for me to find a meaningful job that would enable me to more spend time with my kids. With the support of my husband, I took a well-planned leap out into the world of entrepreneurship. We spent the greater part of a year planning the move and ensuring we could financially and emotionally take it on. We considered different businesses and markets and finally settled on the best opportunity, corporate event planning. It had been one of my responsibilities at my last job, and I truly enjoyed it. Now I go back to my former employer and the executives I used to report to, but this time, as a vendor. It's been a lot of fun.

As the owner and president of my small corporate and special events firm, I leverage everything I've learned from my previous female managers. These incredibly smart and capable women showed me how to organize, influence, persuade, write, and go above and beyond to get the job done right. They too were excited to take on new challenges and tackle new opportunities. Now, I have the chance to continue on as they would, but with my own unique style and environment.

I set up shop at a great location within my town center so I could be close to school and home. I chose an office outside the house because I couldn't see myself balancing conference calls and employee meetings with competing laundry and cooking duties. Also, I'd learned from one of my earliest female mentors at Unilever that close proximity between office and home is key if you want a shot at being involved in your kids' lives while having a career. From the time we planned to have children, my husband and I scoped out the nearest suburb with top schools, and we've been here ever since.

In this new career, I look back with gratitude and appreciation for the skills I gained by being in such an aggressive and challenging corporate environment. Running a business efficiently wouldn't be possible without those skills. Keeping that appreciation in mind, I love tweaking the traditional ways of working to accommodate a more flexible work environment while still adding value to my clients' worlds. Increasing sales and creating effective marketing plans are now the things that push me out of my comfort zone. I get an adrenaline rush from selling to a new client or creating an exciting new event. The fact that I can still have these exciting new opportunities while being a working mother is what I've been striving for.

As my business continues to grow, I get to recruit talented and diverse women. Some are former professional women who decided to stay home for their children. Now that their kids are full-time school age, they seek to work in an environment that is professional, meaningful, and creative, but highly flexible. They get to accept or deny projects of varying roles and length and they relish having options. Many take the school holidays and summer vacations off, which works well for their families, but also for the ebb and flow of our event schedules. It's a perfect fit.

I also recruit talented young women who aren't yet married or have kids. These women are offered different flexibility. They're not local to New Jersey where my business is based, so I provide the option to work from their homes and only commute into the office two days a week to connect with the team or commute to event sites as needed. While they don't have the same commitments in their personal lives as the other working mothers on our team, they appreciate not driving in rush hour traffic and having extra time for personal hobbies.

During my first year in business, I was interviewed by a blogger who focuses on working moms. She wanted to understand the type of company I was creating. It was the first time I realized that I didn't just create a flexible environment for myself, I created it for all the ladies that work on the team. It was a proud moment for me. I have the best of both work and motherhood, and I get the best of these women who otherwise wouldn't be out in the working world. This has become the most rewarding part of my new business. These women have balance, flexibility, and truly enjoy the events and projects they work on. That balance and freedom gives them a much better mindset while working in the office. They're focused and efficient.

And while I've truly enjoyed creating this thriving business, I still need to work on improving how I maintain overall balance. Four and a half years in, it's still hard to do it all. As my children get older and encounter more complex social issues with friends and classmates and have more challenging schoolwork, I need to be there for them even more. My daughter is two years older than my twins, and having three kids so close in age requires as much energy as I can muster. I've learned to put the laptop and phone away at key times. I've trained myself to go back to my emails when the homework is done, the games are over, and they're settled in for the night. This makes for longer nights for me, but I'm OK with that. This schedule allows me to be fulfilled as a mother and as a business owner, so it's a small price to pay. I'm not claiming to be perfect. I need to be more disciplined about not making this a seven-nights-per-week habit, and I continually strive to be a better partner to my husband, a dearer friend, and take better care of myself physically and emotionally. As I vowed when I returned from India, I will continually strive to make the lives around me better for having me in them. It's the biggest challenge I've ever taken on. This year I've promised to empower my team more, be less controlling, take care of my health, and stop to smell the roses more with my kids before they're all grown up and off to college. I will give back to my community and to the people I encounter.

I recently had the opportunity to work on a charity event for ALS research in New York City. It was a new challenge for my team and for me. We had to set up a foreign charity here in the U.S. and work with New York City to create a 400-person swim event in the Hudson River. After the swim, there was a festival on the pier for thousands of supporters. Every day presented new challenges, which gave me renewed energy and motivation in everything I did at work and home. I had a personal association with the disease as my aunt passed away from ALS years ago. Now I had the opportunity to help the cause while creating value for my client and growing as a professional along the way. I included my husband, children, and extended family in every step of the way so they could understand what I was working to achieve. As the charity's president was speaking on stage, he acknowledged me directly, in front of thousands of people. Standing in the audience with my children, husband, and colleagues, I was elated. Not to be recognized in public, but to see the faces of my children when I received the recognition. The nine months of endless work and sleepless nights were worth every second when I saw them beaming. They were truly proud of what their mother accomplished. I was too.

So here's the advice I can offer to other women about redefining success and perhaps considering their own step into small business ownership:

First, choose a profession that makes you truly happy. The work you do needs to provide real satisfaction and accomplishment beyond providing a paycheck. Otherwise, the effort and potential sacrifices aren't worth it. As we all learn eventually, life is too short not to enjoy the ride.

Second, adopt a mindset for giving back as you build your new business or career. Whether that's something you can do with your colleagues, clients, or community, the satisfaction of providing value will give you the extra motivation needed to keep going when it gets hard, because it will get hard.

Finally, and most importantly, be open to change. Pushing yourself in new directions will always provide positive rewards. The most successful women I know have transformed themselves as life changed. These women are lawyers turned yoga instructors, corporate marketers turned chefs, big city hospital doctors turned small practice physicians. They all look back with a fond appreciation of the professional or the stay-at-home moms that they once were while embracing the next version of themselves. I too am enjoying the journey of morphing myself from my past careers into my current business reality. I'm equally excited to see what changes I bring into my life and my family as we grow. The possibilities are endless if you choose to uncover them.

A note from Sarah and Ally: It's hard to let go of that image in the cargo plane, isn't it? Or traveling through Russia, working to conquer the language and take the world by storm, or standing on one of the highest peaks on the planet? Melanie is one of the adventurers in our book, and we feel lucky to have her share her insights with us through her chapter.

There is a theme running through Melanie's story: Life is going to change, but it's up to us to use those changes to make ourselves stronger, kinder, and more caring. At each step in her life, she could have pushed harder, and maybe allowed herself to become harder, but she didn't. She followed her heart and her intuition and she gave life permission to shape her into the business owner and woman she is today.

As we learned from Orna's story, it could be said that we all have a responsibility to bring the best of ourselves to everything we do. Melanie embodies that in her company, MDC Event Group. She created a new path for herself, and by doing so she's created opportunity, employment, and growth for other women.

Melanie dances with every turn life gives her, and she uses each new chapter to her advantage by creating a better solution and bringing other women along with her. Her recent ALS event is the perfect example of how she's learned to make herself happy while paying it forward at the same time. Success is best when it's shared and passed on.

Chapter Challenge

What part of Melanie's story could you relate to the most?

_____

_____

If you could name only one thing you took away from this story, what would it be?

_____

_____

_____

What one thing will you do differently because of Melanie's story?

_____

_____

What surprised you the most in this story?

_____

_____

_____

If there was one thing you could ask Melanie, what would it be?

_____

_____

We'd love for you to connect with Melanie. If you'd like to connect with her, simply send an email to info@redefiningsuccessstories.com and put Melanie's name in the subject line.

WE'RE STRONGER TOGETHER

Mariel Alvarado & Brandyn Coe Randolph

When women decide to work together, there's nothing that can stand in our way.

How do two ladies from Texas, now living in New Jersey, end up building their dream tribe and their dream business? Well, we would love to tell you a story about how we strategically and meticulously planned everything, but that would be a lie. We would love to say that we're networking goddesses, digital marketing queens, and tech savvy millennials, but the truth is we were just two bored mommies. We built Lady Savant Society, a sisterhood and members' club for entrepreneurial women, by exploring, messing up, and step by step, in between nap times, hard times, good times, pregnancies and by always asking each other "What if we..."

In the summer of 2012 our vision for Lady Savant Society was born as we were covered in paint and sawdust, in the throes of our new hobby: painting furniture. Painting furniture was our way of "exploring." It started as a hobby meant to give us a break from the daily grind of being stay-at-home moms. But as we developed and worked on this hobby, we found ourselves thinking:

"What if there was a group of women who were soulful, entrepreneurial, and a little crazy, like us, who supported each other, learned from each other, bought from each other, and were committed to each other's growth as women and in business? Is that even possible?"

It was the first of many "What if..." moments that made us put our paintbrushes down and veer out into the future to build a brand-new community. We didn't know much about networking or social media or websites, and looking back, that was a good thing. But we had a vision and the rest was the universe conspiring in our favor, every step of the way. In fact, it still is!

Lady Savant Comes Together

Mariel: My mom always says, "God makes them and they will find each other," and that's how I feel about Brandyn and me. We always say the universe was conspiring for us to meet way before we met. In the summer of 2007, Brandyn and her husband, Trevor, met my partner, Bobby, in Puerto Rico while they were on vacation. Bobby was there for a bachelor party. They hung out all weekend and about a year later, we all met back in New Jersey at a brunch on a Sunday morning. It was the first time Brandyn and I met, and we immediately hit it off. We talked all morning about our similarities, and the fact that neither of us had many friends in New Jersey. We discovered that we're both from Houston, Texas, had boys the same age, and had even given birth in the same hospital in New York City. Our bond grew stronger and a few months later, Brandyn and Trevor moved to a new house, just two houses away from ours.

So there we were, two bored mommies from Texas with hardly any friends in New Jersey, struggling to get back to being "ourselves." We were used to working outside the home and making our own money, but also to having goals outside of our families. Everything we ever knew was so different now that we were home. We had both wanted to be home with our kids, but it's not easy. We never anticipated feeling so lost. Being the new moms in town can be quite lonely and boring. There's only so much going to the gym, lunch, or play dates one person can handle. It's almost like we lost part of ourselves and couldn't quite explain it. And we never wanted to sound ungrateful. We were happy to be home, but there was more for us to do, and we knew it. Thank God for the early days of companionship and friendship.

Brandyn: When my first son was born, I continued working part-time at the staffing agency where I'd been working for four years. It was a great arrangement for me. I had my time to be out in the world and be the woman I'd always been, and still be home with my first little boy. Two years later, baby boy number two came along, and it just didn't make sense to work anymore. That's when I became a full-time stay-at-home mom and my life changed dramatically.

I tend to think the grass is greener on the other side, and I was definitely experiencing that when I decided to stay home full-time. When I'd been working, I dreamed of staying home, but now that I was home, I dreamed of working again and seeing my friends on a daily basis. I missed the structure and knowing what tomorrow would bring. I was the first of my local friends to have kids, so it was quite an adjustment. I didn't have anyone to have play dates with and no one to talk about being a mom. I wanted to get out of the house and do something creative again. I wasn't sure exactly what, but changing diapers all day, cleaning up spilled milk, and repeating, "Don't do that" to my toddler got old, quickly. My husband worked long hours and my family lived in Texas so I was going through a mix of emotions. One minute I was extremely content and then the next, depressed and lost. I would think, "Why am I feeling this way? I wanted to be a stay-at-home mom."

Of course my husband tried to understand what I was going through,

196

but there is no way he could fully understand until he could experience what it is like to be at home all day with two toddlers. As other mothers know, it's one of the toughest jobs a person will ever do, and it's a job that *never* ends. As I was struggling with all of this, Trevor suggested I get some help with the boys for a few hours, a couple of days a week and go find a hobby. A hobby? What's a hobby? I never had a hobby! I'd always worked and I never had the time or the resources to have hobbies. I expressed my frustration to my family, and my older sister, Kendra, inspired me to try something new. She had gone through the same feelings when she was a new mother, and her daughter was now three. She took up a hobby restoring and painting old furniture and turned it into a little business. I remember seeing the excitement and passion when she spoke about painting and the unique furniture she would find online or in thrift stores. I wanted that same passion, but I had no idea where to start. I thought, "I can't do that. I'm not crafty or creative. I can't even color inside the lines!" Then one day I got the courage to try, and I fell in love with it.

I brought my best friend, neighbor, and now partner of Lady Savant, Mariel in on the secret. We created our own small business called "Soulfully Chic." We had so much fun spending weekends picking up old furniture from craigslist and bringing it home to paint. Oh, the stories we could tell you! We sold our pieces on Etsy and craigslist, and that's how it all started. Thanks to websites like Pinterest and Etsy, inspiring ideas were right at our fingertips. Painting not only brought out our creative sides, it made us feel like we could do something outside of motherhood or working behind a computer. There is nothing more rewarding than sharing what you've created with someone who falls in love with your work and buys it. This was our fix! I was finally becoming happy and content again. Then one afternoon I had a vision: a local marketplace of women buying, referring, and helping each other in business. I remember sharing my idea with Mariel and then she spun other ideas off that and the rest is history. We were on fire and nothing was going to slow us down.

That is until I was surprised with pregnancy number three. I had always wanted three children, but not this soon. We were just starting our second business and I was incredibly excited about it. Now I was faced with the dilemma of "leaning in" or waiting until after the baby was born and I was settled again. I decided to lean in. Although the first couple of months were brutal, as in most pregnancies, I decided this was as good as any other time to start. After all, we all have to start some time, and today is always better than tomorrow.

Mariel: More often than not, as we women enter motherhood and start caring for someone else so completely, we start to ignore our own needs. Especially when those needs aren't visible. Not all of our needs are physical, and many times, it's the non-physical needs that are easiest to ignore. For example, everyone needs love, companionship, and to find their calling in life. But it's so easy to put those needs on the back burner, especially when caring for someone else. It's effortless to ignore our innermost needs, at least in the beginning. Becoming a mother was definitely a calling for Brandyn and me, but it wasn't the only one.

When we started painting furniture I started feeling a lot better and finally felt like I had a direction again. It wasn't even that painting furniture was going to be a moneymaker. It was about sitting down and imagining something and making it happen with our own hands. It's quite a powerful experience! I was hooked, not only because I enjoyed the painting so much, but because I loved using my creative muscles, probably for the first time ever. Besides being someone who appreciates art and fashion, I had no idea I had this creative side to me.

Brandyn and I were very lucky to have each other. It isn't easy finding a partner in crime, the yin to your yang. And it isn't easy to figure out what you want in general. In retrospect, part of the reason we were so gutsy and tried new things was because we had each other. Every time one of us said "What if we..." we had an immediate sounding board; someone receptive that didn't think the new ideas were ridiculous. Everyone should be lucky enough to have a friend who conspires with you to reach and find your dreams. This was one of the reasons Lady Savant Society was created.

We didn't spend our time gossiping about people or talking about motherhood. I mean, there have been many days and nights where tears flowed, frustrations dug in, and doubts gnawed at us. But overall, we spent our time asking each other "What if we..." and the rest of the time figuring out how to make it happen. Our mission with Lady Savant Society was to create a real sisterhood of entrepreneurial women supporting each other personally and professionally.

During this time of reinvention, I was also searching individually and I found a long-lost friend who had started a group on morningcoach.com. I signed up for his inspiring daily podcasts and was motivated to move forward. I also learned how to meditate, which was a game-changer for me. Combining these things helped clear my head and keep me focused. I realized I didn't want to make motherhood or being a stay-at-home mom an excuse for not doing what I wanted to do. My partner, Bobby, an entrepreneur himself, was extremely supportive. I had no excuse to not make my dreams a reality.

I became an entrepreneur when I was 23 years old. I've always gone my own way. I'm originally from Texas, and I'm Mexican. I'm the oldest of four, and the only girl. After graduating college with degrees in Communications and Marketing, I moved to Miami with my now ex-husband and met an amazing woman who trained me in direct sales and taught me how to become my own boss. In this role I learned to train, motivate, and lead a team. This position undoubtedly turned me into an inspiration junkie and an entrepreneur. To this day, I believe in setting goals and seeking inspiration on a daily basis.

A year and a half later I relocated to Chicago, where I opened my first business: an outsourced direct sales office. I was hired by a fortune 500 Company to build their direct marketing sales teams, as in "door-to-door" sales teams. Yep, a peddler myself, I was now the queen of the peddlers. It was fun. I was young, good at my work, and I was doing well for myself. A year later I got divorced and moved back to Miami to open up a second office. But the thrill of being a new entrepreneur was slowly fading away. By my third year in business there, I was burnt out. I started to feel the burden of the responsibility that came with having employees and overhead. I decided it was time to relax and give corporate America a shot. So I took an advertising job in New York City. Then I moved to New Jersey with my better half, Bobby, whom I had met and dated for two years while I was still living in Miami. When our son Little

Bobby was born, I decided to stay at home with him.

I wouldn't change anything about those early years. When I lived in Florida I had very strong female mentors. One of those mentors was Julie Edmonds, an entrepreneur and author of *The Six Questions: That You Better Get Right, The Answers are the Keys to Your Success*. She guided me and taught me everything I needed to know to open up my first marketing business in Chicago. I will always be grateful for Julie's friendship and guidance. I was also very close to a woman named Omian, a very special soul. She's the most spiritual, wisest woman I've ever met. Do you remember the Oracle in *The Matrix*? Omian was like that, times ten. She took me under her wing for many years and taught me "The Way of Spirit," which was her very own Christian spiritual movement. Every Sunday she taught a class in her home and no matter how late a Saturday night I had, I never missed her Sunday mornings. They were spiritual lessons for those of us who have never been too fond of organized religion.

A year after leaving Miami, I was sitting in my office in New York City on a Thursday morning when I suddenly felt the urge to go to Miami for the weekend. I followed the urge, got a ticket, and decided to take the next day and Monday off from work. I really wanted to see Omian, and it was so refreshing to spend time with her over the weekend. I went to her Sunday morning class, took her and her husband out for breakfast on Monday, and flew back Monday night.

202

The next day, I got the phone call that she had mysteriously passed away in her sleep. It was the most surreal thing that had ever happened to me. I was her last student to see her alive. It was like my soul knew she was leaving. From that day forward, I promised myself never to ignore that little inner voice. In fact, that was part of her teachings, part of living in "The Way of Spirit" as she called it. My life has not been the same since her loss. I miss her every single day.

However, Omian's teachings are very much alive in me. She taught me that true success is something that happens on three levels: body, mind, and spirit. There is no lasting happiness or success unless those three are aligned. She loved butterflies, which is why we have butterfly wings on our Lady Savant logo. Her influence is always with me and therefore with Lady Savant.

I believe many women feel isolated and confused about their needs during transitional times, like those early years of motherhood. Not everyone has friends that understand, or even a support system, and sometimes our biggest fears are not what our family or our partners think, but what other women think. In those early days of motherhood, I would go to mommy meet-ups and various mommy web forums, and it never failed to amaze me how worried I would get about being judged by complete strangers. It's become my goal to move the dialogue between women to a new level of grace, support, and acceptance. Whether you are a new mom, a divorcee, a person that has recently lost their job, an empty nester, or whatever your situation may be, you need to find what makes *you* happy.

Being a woman today, and all that entails, is not easy. There is a lot of juggling involved if you want to "have it all." We know that being an entrepreneur can be very lonely and seeing other women walk the walk is a *must* if you want to succeed. Who you become in five years boils down to the books you read and the people you surround yourself with. Our mission at Lady Savant Society is for women entrepreneurs to come together to share knowledge, create collaborations, develop friendships, make memories, and build support systems. Every woman should envision her story, explore life with friends, and evolve into the woman she wants to be because anything and everything is possible *if you have a vision* and your vision expands when you surround yourself with like-minded women.

Your ideas and vision are important and valuable and the thing is, somebody out there *will* do it if you don't. So why shouldn't it be you? There is no such thing as a new idea, everything has been thought of at one point or another by someone. It's about *execution*. Are you willing to do something about your idea? Are you willing to be yourself? If you can imagine it and believe it, you can achieve it. Your reward will come when you create the capacity to receive it.

Being part of a sisterhood of like-minded entrepreneurial women helps women create the capacity to receive support, ideas, knowledge, friendship, and business. That is why we love our business so much. There is nothing more fulfilling than to see other women get to the next level!

A note from Sarah and Ally: So there's a little secret you should probably know: Ally and Sarah met at a Lady Savant event a few years ago. If it weren't for the community of women that Mariel and Brandyn created, this book wouldn't be in your hands. As we learned in Melanie's story, when we listen to our intuition and follow our hearts, we invariably bring other women along with us. Mariel and Brandyn are doing that in a very direct way, but the side effects of their partnership will continue to bring new and amazing creations into the world. And while they're bringing women together to share, none of us can have any idea what's truly possible until we see it start to happen.

What we love so much about their story, aside from how clearly they love each other, is that they created an answer to their own problem. Most moms can relate to Brandyn's experience of motherhood, and the sense of "Hey, where did I go?" that can happen as we turn our full attention to children. But both Mariel and Brandyn allowed themselves to dream about what could be possible, and they supported each other as they moved into their new roles in life. They worked hard, but learned to dance with the opportunities and connections that were offered to them; which is a theme we've seen consistently throughout this book.

What Mariel touches upon as she shares her story about Omian and listening to the prompt to go see her, is crucial to success. What we women have in spades is our intuition. As young girls, we may have lost touch with that small voice, and some of us may not even hear it anymore. The good news is, the more we listen, the stronger it becomes. As women in business, and in life, our success relies heavily upon our ability to trust our own judgments, to listen to ourselves first, and then to take in what others may need from us. It's the opposite from what most of us do, but it's something we can all strive for as we reach towards success.

Chapter Challenge

What part of the Savant Ladies' story could you relate to the most?

_____

_____

If you could name only one thing you took away from this story, what would it be?

_____

_____

_____

What one thing will you do differently because of their story?

_____

_____

What surprised you the most in this story?

_____

_____

_____

If there was one thing you could ask Mariel or Brandyn, what would it be?

_____

_____

We'd love for you to connect with Mariel & Brandyn. If you'd like to connect with them, simply send an email with their names in the subject line to info@redefiningsuccessstories.com.

SOME SERIOUS GRATITUDE

Books usually end with a list of people the author wants to thank, or maybe even an update on the story that's just been finished. For all 14 of us, and our 13 stories, the list would be so long we'd have a whole other book to write. But if you've ever sat down and tried to write about your own life, or about your failures and successes, you can imagine what it took to get 14 women to sit down at a computer and get this done. It was a wild, fun, exciting ride and we want to sincerely thank *you* for taking part in it by reading it.

To start, we want to thank each of our authors for being brave enough to tell the truth; to talk about things people don't always want to talk about; to share their battle scars in the hopes that others will take heart, have courage, and know that no woman is alone. We're all in this together, even when we can't see each other. There is a silent bond in womanhood. We experience it when we share a knowing smile while waiting in line at the grocery store; when we hold the door for each other, experience childbirth, or hold a baby; when we mentor a co-worker, train a new hire, care for a sick child, or show up at a friend's house when we have a feeling they need us.

We hope this book will be your reminder of that bond, of our shared courage, love, and strength, and that you remember it when times are hard and you're discouraged, as well as when times are amazing and you're feeling on top of the world. Both of those experiences are equally important, and the more we connect over them, the stronger we all become. None of us can make it through life without bruises and scrapes, and ultimately, it's the difficult moments that give birth to our greatest ones, if we choose to learn from them and grasp the opportunity.

There are the usual suspects we'd like to thank for their support and love: our significant others, business partners, our children, friends, and close family who've been patient as we cried through our first few drafts, paced with nervousness, typed into the wee hours of the morning, and edited our pieces on vacation, over the phone, and late at night. It's no small feat to coordinate 14 women, and we couldn't have done it without the army of love that stands behind us. There are also several baristas and waiters that we'd like to give a shout-out to for making sure were fed and caffeinated at local coffee shops as we hemmed and hawed over word choices, sentence structure, and deleted paragraphs. And last but not least, our copy editor Marcia Abramson, our cover designer Dan Halpern and our illustrator Agung "Konco".

And then there are the not-so-usual suspects that we'd like to thank: the people in the stories we've shared; the experiences that shaped us, stretched us, and challenged us; the angels who helped us write down what we wanted to say, and the women who've come before us and paved the way when there was no way.

As we move through life, we'll be told what we should want, what we should wear, who we should be, and what should make us happy. At each turn, it's up to us to choose whether or not we let those messages in, or if we choose to take the time to sit down and really craft our own visions of success and move on from there. There is no success without happiness, and it's our responsibility and privilege to design what that means.

With our sincerest gratitude and love we say: Redefine success for yourself, then go out there and make it happen.

Made in the USA
Middletown, DE
24 September 2015